COUNSELLING

COUNSELLING
A SKILLS APPROACH

E.A. Munro

R.J. Manthei

J.J. Small

Methuen
New Zealand

First published in 1979.
Revised edition published in 1983 by
Methuen Publications (N.Z.) Ltd,
61 Beach Road, Auckland.

ISBN 0 456 03130 8

Cover illustration by Dexter Fry

Typeset by Computype Services Ltd, Wellington
Printed in Hong Kong by Wing King Tong Co. Ltd

Contents

Foreword to the Second Edition

This book expresses again our belief that counselling, the process of helping others, can be described as a series of skills and stages, governed by some important ethical principles. We reaffirm our belief that these skills and principles are of general value and that they should be more widely known and practised. The book has been written with a minimum of technical terms, and is intended for counsellors working in various settings (educational, vocational, medical, social, and rehabilitative) and for those offering training courses for such counsellors.

In some chapters the counsellor is consistently referred to as 'he' and the client as 'she'. In others this pattern is reversed. This was done both to simplify the presentation within chapters and to express our commitment to the equality of the sexes.

Each of the authors has shared equally in revising the book and thus each accepts equal responsibility for its contents. The order of authorship does not indicate any difference in contributions. Collectively we have been able to draw upon many years of experience in counselling research and in the study, teaching, and practice of counselling, mainly in New Zealand, but also in Australia, England and the United States. Each of us has been enriched by the sharing of these experiences with our teachers, colleagues, students and clients. To all these people we are very grateful. We would appreciate comments and suggestions from them and from others.

We wish to acknowledge the use of the following references: J. Luft, *Of Human Interaction,* Palo Alto, CA: Mayfield Publishing, 1969 (exercise p. 22); D.W. Johnson, *Reaching Out,* Englewood Cliffs, N.J.: Prentice Hall, 1972 (exercise p. 52); *Prevention* (December, 1977, Rodale Press, Emmaus, PA (exercise pp. 85-86); R.J. Manthei and D.A. Matthews, Helping the reluctant client to engage in counselling, *British Journal of Guidance and Counselling,* 1982, *10,* pp. 44-50 (included here with the permission of the publishers, CRAC/Hobsons Press, Bateman St., Cambridge CB2 1LZ, England) (text pp. 46-49).

Anne Munro
Bob Manthei
John Small

1

Introduction

The purpose of this book is to describe how people can improve their methods of helping others to understand themselves better and to be more effective in solving their problems. The term 'counselling' is used here to cover the various skills and principles of helping. The setting within which these skills are described is a face-to-face relationship between two people – counsellor and client. However, the skills and principles of individual counselling (sometimes called casework) are directly applicable in other settings as well. These include family counselling, various kinds of group work, and aspects of social work, teaching, supervision, and administration. One other important area in which casework skills can be applied is consultation, in which a counsellor helps a professional to deal with a work-related problem.

In any counselling relationship the expert counsellor has at his disposal a range of methods of helping clients. Each method counts as counselling when certain other conditions of the relationship are met. These conditions are of an ethical nature and include the following: a higher degree of confidentiality than is normally expected of, say, teachers; an insistence on the voluntary nature of the relationship; and an emphasis on the personal responsibility of the client for her own behaviour. Moreover, the counsellor, while being responsible for his own behaviour and interested in his client's welfare, does not allow the counselling relationship with his client to be compromised by any other relationship he might have with her, such as supervisor or friend.

Like related activities such as teaching, administering, or leading others, the ability to counsel may seem somewhat mysterious. But it should not be regarded as a mystique or a special charisma bestowed upon only a few individuals. It is true that some people are effective counsellors without having studied counselling systematically. They seem to have an intuitive knack for saying and doing the most helpful thing at the right time, and to have personal attributes that enhance their effectiveness. A good deal remains to be learned about this, but enough progress has been made in studying and teaching the counselling process to justify confidence in describing it as consisting of separate skills. If counselling is to be de-mystified and made more widely available to clients and to counsellors, the first step is to describe the skills of counselling in language that is both clear and non-technical.

This is a central point. There are many possible views of the counselling process, but for learning and teaching purposes it is useful to view it as a series of interactions consisting of certain behaviours by one person which produce certain responses in another. Apart from any judgment that might be made about the quality of a counsellor's overall performance, for instructional purposes it is more helpful to view it in terms of separate behaviours and their effects.

Effective counselling means using different skills at different times. In the early stages of a relationship it is helpful to listen carefully and to respond to the client's overt behaviours and apparent needs. At other times influencing a client by getting her to do something may be more appropriate. Consider, for example, the anxiety which many clients show at various stages of the counselling process. Sometimes the counsellor will purposely ignore the obvious signs of anxiety. At other times he may simply comment upon them openly, but neutrally, and say no more, thus indicating an acceptance of the behaviour. Alternatively, he may decide to reduce the anxiety level so that a freer discussion can take place. Whatever is decided, to be effective the counsellor must have the skill to carry out his intention. Exactly what he does is, of course, a function of his counselling experience, training and knowledge.

In another important sense, however, the primary role of the counsellor is not one of merely using techniques. It is essentially an ethical task. Simply stated, it is to serve the client's best interests. These can be difficult to determine, but the role of servant is central to counselling, for the counsellor's ultimate responsibility is to help people to get what they want, provided that this does not conflct with the counsellor's personal values.

If people show clearly that they do not want help and do not wish to change, the counsellor has no right to impose his views upon them, regardless of his skill, insight, or ability to predict outcomes. Behind this assertion lies an awareness that sometimes the counsellor's need to give help may be as strong as, or even stronger than, the client's need to receive it. As discussed in chapter 2, the counsellor must be knowledgeable not only about others but also about himself.

There are three further ethical considerations. First, the counselling skills described are confined almost exclusively to influencing people through talking. Such techniques as legal coercion, medication, testing, or the use of apparatus or equipment are sometimes regarded as part of counselling. However, because they raise complex issues about the rights of clients and the authority and qualifications of counsellors, these techniques are beyond the scope of this book.

Secondly, since counselling means dealing with people, the skills described are not neutral or value-free in the sense that practical skills are. Counselling of whatever kind is rightly taken to represent a set of beliefs and assumptions about people, about interpersonal relationships, and about ways of influencing others.

Thirdly, when the counsellor and his client are from different cultures (taken here to include differences of sex, age, race, social class and religion, as well as membership in a particular culture), there will be important differences between them in what they expect about their respective roles and about desirable outcomes. It is also likely that the counsellor will need to use different language and skills from those he has found to be effective with clients from his own cultural group. Even more so than in counselling generally, it is vital for the counsellor in a cross-cultural setting to enhance the match between his and his client's expectations about roles, outcomes, and appropriate behaviours.

A skills approach to training can do much to further the possibility of this match occurring. Training in specific skills can equip counsellors with an increased number of verbal and non-verbal responses when communicating to others and an increased sensitivity to cultural variations in communications from others. Also, culturally-specific patterns of relating can be more readily identified and taught to others, using a skills-based approach.

However, much more needs to be done to develop skill and sensitivity in counselling across cultures. It is strongly recommended that all counsellors: (a) become aware of their own cultural values and beliefs, of how these affect their perceptions of other cultural groups, and of how they may conflict with a client's values and beliefs; (b) develop an openness and flexibility toward other cultural groups and an understanding of the political, economic, and social forces affecting those groups; and (c) acquire some basic knowledge about the specific cultural groups they may be working with, e.g., language, customs, values and history. Training experiences to supplement the basic skills training outlined in this book should include: (a) acquisition of basic information about specific cultures; (b) basic language training; (c) role-playing, simulation exercises and case study discussions of cross-cultural counselling situations; and (d) actual contact with members of as many different cultures as possible.

Among the values and assumptions implied in this book are the following:

1. Many people need help in coping with their difficulties.
2. Most people who need help have within themselves some resources for coping which counsellors can elicit.
3. The ability to show such qualities as sincerity, warmth, and empathy is essential for counselling.
4. Counselling is based partly upon rational approaches, partly upon the expression of feelings, and partly upon the assessment of values.
5. While counsellors offer a variety of helping skills, ultimately it is the client who determines the content, the methods, and the success of counselling.

Theory in Counselling

The focus of this book is on counselling as a problem-solving activity. Most counsellors use a variety of skills throughout the counselling process, and these can be conveniently grouped into three main stages. A rationale has been developed for understanding these stages by asking questions about each. What are the best skills to use when entering into a counselling relationship? How should one explore and define issues and problems when counselling? What skills are most useful in helping to resolve and reduce these problems?

This rationale serves as a general theory of intervention, one which views the helping process in terms of stages but avoids certain other commitments. For example, it does not require extensive investigations into causes and factors from the past, although these may be useful in some circumstances. Nor does it depend upon diagnoses such as medical and psychological classifications, although such information may also be useful. In an eclectic fashion it uses skills and principles from various theories of counselling, but it remains uncommitted to any particular one.

There are many counselling theories, and as early as possible in their training counsellors should know the major ones and the many useful techniques and ideas that have been developed within them. But it is virtually impossible to compare theories in terms of their general effectiveness. So far the most careful research has been unable to provide a clear-cut answer to the question: Which theory is best? For counsellors the most relevant question is an equally difficult one: Given this client with these concerns in these circumstances, what should I do now? That immediate and practical question is also a theoretical one, for it implies the ability to justify one's choice, based upon one's knowledge, experience and judgement.

Thus, counselling in its theoretical aspects is best regarded as a procedure based on many kinds of knowledge – the central concepts of the helping process, the effects of different techniques, an appreciation of subjective factors, an understanding of human development, and knowledge about society. When counsellors theorise, these are the sorts of knowledge they should use. Counsellors are in fact theorising in this way when, for example, they are trying to decide whether it is possible to help a particular client, how to understand her, what method to use, or why progress is blocked.

Counsellors need not only this kind of knowledge, but also, as already stated, knowledge of particular theories of counselling. These theories can provide new perspectives on clients' problems and suggest different ways for counsellors to help. In practice, most counsellors use ideas from several different theories, according to how they assess clients' needs at the time. During a full training course, or soon after brief introductory training, all counsellors should study a number of different theories. They would then have to learn how to integrate aspects of these theories into their own counselling repertoire and personal style.

A first step in theorising could be for counsellors to think critically about the skills and principles in this book and the reasons offered in support of them. Careful reading of other books on counselling and on related subjects will lead to further ability to theorise. Theoretical study must also be integrated with practice. Counsellors should therefore reflect on their own counselling experiences, discuss their work with other counsellors, undergo professional supervision, and seek further training opportunities.

Rationale and Outline

This book has been written in the belief that people will become better able to help others if they read it, reflect on it, work at the exercises (if possible in groups guided by an experienced leader), and try to put the ideas into practice. Working to acquire the skills should lead counsellors to become more aware of their own assets and limitations as counsellors, more perceptive of the needs of others and better able to help them, and more sensitive to the finer points of communication and the helping processes. The greatest improvement will occur if the practice of the skills is supervised.

Those who undertake counselling should commit themselves to learning as much as possible about the factors involved in the process. These factors fall into two main categories – subjective personal knowledge, and objective knowledge in the form of useful principles.

Personal factors are crucial in counselling relationships. Mechanical, perfunctory counselling is seldom effective and may even adversely affect a client. It is possible to act out a counselling role, pretending to possess qualities that one does not actually have. Sooner or later most clients sense such a pose, and when they do, whatever technical skill the counsellor might have is likely to be lessened or even negated by client resistance.

To be fully effective the counsellor needs a heightened awareness of his own inner life, including bodily feelings, emotional reactions, preferences, biases, hunches, and intuitions. Such subjective awareness is often regarded as misleading, inaccurate, and even dangerous. But since an inner life is necessarily a part of every person, it is more sensible for each counsellor to come to terms with it. Chapter 2 suggests ways to begin this self-exploration and provides exercises to assist counsellors in knowing themselves better.

In chapters 3, 4 and 5 specific counselling skills are described. These have been drawn from two main sources: recent research and developments in counsellor training; and our own varied experiences both as counsellors and counsellor trainers. If there is one word which best expresses our ideas about the training of counsellors, it is 'micro-counselling', the identification of small steps or skills in counselling for study, practice, and application.

Each of these central chapters deals with one of the three main stages or phases in a counselling relationship – the beginning phase, the developing phase, and the behaviour-change phase. Within each stage, separate skills have been described, exemplified, and explained. Exercises enable counsellors to practise a skill immediately after reading about it, and where answers are given at the end of the book, the exercise is marked with an asterisk. Not all of the skills will be used in any one counselling relationship, nor do the stages always occupy the amount or proportion of counselling time that might be implied by the presentation. Counselling often occurs in a much more condensed fashion. Nevertheless the elaboration of stages and skills provides a wide range of approaches which can then be used flexibly.

Chapter 6 shows how counselling skills could be made more widely available in the community through teaching and consultation. Success in passing these skills on to others depends greatly upon the counsellor first having acquired and practised the skills himself, but there are also a number of practical considerations. Suggestions are made about conducting a group, and supervision is also discussed.

Finally, in chapter 7 other issues are considered. Several value questions are examined; counselling in groups and other settings is discussed; guides for assessing progress and effectiveness are suggested; and the principles of supervision are presented.

Summary

Counselling is a way of helping others by using a variety of skills and principles within a relationship that is subject to certain ethical and value requirements. In this book individual casework is the focus for discussing the various skills and principles, but these skills are also relevant to helping in other settings such as with groups and in various professional settings.

2
The Counsellor is a Person

In any interpersonal situation, whether group or individual, in which one person assumes the role of 'counsellor', that person also assumes a responsibility for her own behaviour, her knowledge of herself, and her ability to relate effectively to another. Anyone who undertakes to be a counsellor must be prepared to interact as a real person with the client and to strive for an awareness of the factors involved in the process. As it is impossible for a counsellor to be totally objective and rational, anyone who strives to be so denies herself a most valuable source of counselling information – her own feelings, perceptions, hunches and ideas.

Maximum use must be made of all sources of counselling information. This means that the counsellor must rely not only on her perceptions of and understanding of the client's situation as it is related to her, but also on her own feelings about and reactions to what is happening at the time. This latter source is often purposely ignored because it is thought that subjective impressions are necessarily inaccurate and biased. They are, however, potentially the more accurate of the two types of information, provided the counsellor can develop her self-awareness to a level that will enable her accurately to identify and interpret her own reactions and feelings. By contrast, her understanding of another person's situation is always diminished by the fact that any communication from one person to another is prone to some degree of distortion and error. Counselling can be thought of as a dynamic relationship involving two people, and one in which the counsellor's knowledge of herself is as important as the knowledge of the client and of counselling principles.

This dynamic relationship is a process of defining and redefining the specific roles that the counsellor and client will play. Participants can decide *how* to respond to one another, but not *whether* they will respond. For example, in any encounter with another person, everything said or done communicates to the other person how one is willing to relate. If someone says, 'I don't understand what we are supposed to be doing', any response (verbal or non-verbal) by another person begins to define a relationship between them. How would each of these responses to the statement above begin to define a relationship?

1. 'I don't either. Let's ask someone else.'
2. 'Maybe you should listen more.'
3. 'I don't either. What should we do?'
4. Shrug of the shoulders.
5. Say nothing, merely turn away from the person.
6. 'Let me see if I can find out for you, OK?'
7. 'We are supposed to be reading pages 46-52.'

In the first example, the respondent refuses to assume a leadership or information-giver's role and instead becomes an equal by admitting her ignorance and suggesting that both ask someone else. In the second example, a critical, distant position is assumed that clearly indicates the respondent does not want the speaker to become dependent on her in any way. In (3), after admitting she does not know, the respondent refuses to accept a leadership role and instead tries to get the speaker to take over or at least recognise that they both have some responsibility for solving the problem. The shrug will probably be interpreted as, 'Don't ask me; I don't want to get involved', indicating a desire for no further interaction. The action in (5), no matter how it is done, clearly indicates the respondent's desire for non-involvement. Example (6) illustrates the respondent's willingness to accept a supportive leadership role. The final example gives the information required but probably leaves the speaker undecided about whether further interaction can occur.

This same process of defining and redefining a relationship occurs in counselling. Every word, gesture, and silence alters how the counsellor and client will relate while together.

The Counsellor's Needs in Counselling

Before seriously considering herself a counsellor, each person should critically and honestly examine her own motivations for taking on the responsibilities of helping another person. Very simply, she should ask herself: 'What do I expect from the relationship? What will be my satisfactions and rewards in helping others?'

A counsellor's reasons for helping are seldom entirely pure and altruistic, but every counsellor should be open to and aware of her motivations. After all, these motivations can profoundly influence her effectiveness. The counsellor who helps others in order to avoid dealing with her own problems will be limited in her effectiveness. Even if clients do not 'see through' her in a completely accurate way, they will never develop the confidence and trust in her that is essential if she is to help them effectively. Similarly, the counsellor who encourages her clients to confide in her because it gives her status and control will soon find that she will have only one type of client, as others will avoid her and her controlling behaviour.

Some counsellors may desire close contact with others but be unable to achieve these relationships in normal interpersonal situations. By becoming counsellors they are able to avoid facing up to their own deficiencies and to feel competent and fulfilled in working closely with others. There are other counsellors who firmly believe they have answers to life's problems that should be shared with others. With the best of intentions they try to convert clients to their way of thinking but end up alienating many. Others counsel out of a sincere wish to help, with no other hidden motivation. Very often they are unaware of their own rewards and satisfactions. They may be viewed with some scepticism and distrust by the more suspicious or cynical client. Whatever the reasons for helping others, the counsellor's credibility and, hence, her effectiveness will be enhanced by her awareness and acceptance of those reasons.

The first reasons that come to mind might not always be the most honest or accurate. Self-deception in this area hinders effectiveness and, as suggested earlier, *real* motives will be quickly perceived by clients. Adolescents are particularly quick to 'see through' the phoney adult or the counsellor who is only enforcing the school rules in a 'softer' way. Discovering her needs and motivations involves the counsellor in an ongoing examination of her beliefs about herself, her beliefs about others, and her commitment to learning more about herself. Questions she needs to answer are:

1. Who am I?
2. What are my strengths? Weaknesses?
3. What do I need from others?

4. What do I have to offer other people?
5. What do I believe is right for others?

Answering such questions is often difficult and may be painful. However, an effective counsellor should continually strive to know herself. Counsellors must be committed to continuous personal growth both in training and real life situations, and must have the courage and confidence to undertake the in-depth personal analysis they ask of clients. It must be stressed that personal development is an on-going process, and that as a person changes, the questions above will require new answers. It will be necessary for the counsellor periodically to answer the questions, 'Should I be a counsellor? Why?' and also to recognise that her readiness or suitability to counsel will vary as her own circumstances change. There will be times when she will have to sort out her own difficulties before she can resume counselling others. The important thing to recognise is that increased awareness of herself and her motives will enable her to work more effectively with others.

Exercise 2.1

1. Discuss with four or five others your reasons for wanting to become a counsellor. Afterwards, evaluate your participation. How open, searching and honest were you in your statements about yourself? Did you hold back some reasons and instead say what you felt was safe and acceptable? How did others feel about your degree of openness?
2. In pairs, complete the following sentences:
   As a counsellor or helper –
   (a) I am becoming the kind of person who . . .
   (b) My strengths are . . .
   (c) My weaknesses are . . .
   (d) What I need most from people is . . .
   (e) What I give to people most of the time is . . .
   When both people have completed these statements, discuss the following questions in the larger group:
   (a) How open, searching and honest were you in your statements about yourself?
   (b) Which statements were the easiest to complete? Most difficult? Why?
   (c) What did you learn about yourself?

3. Using the information and self-knowledge gained from the exercises above, write a one-page statement of your present motivations to be a counsellor. The last sentence should be an assessment of how honest and open you believe your statement to be. Keep this statement and refer to it frequently as you progress through this book or your training course. Alter and amend your statement at any time you wish. Do not share your statement with others unless you want to do so.

Developing Self-awareness

A preliminary step in developing overall self-awareness involves counsellors experiencing and enjoying their inner and external worlds through the senses. In the following exercises, try to be open to new sensations and feelings without controlling or analysing them. Be relaxed and receptive to whatever happens.

EXERCISE 2.2

To experience awareness through the various senses:

1. Close your eyes and sit quietly in a comfortable position. As you begin to relax become aware of all the sounds around you. Gradually become aware of sounds within you. Discuss your experience with others.
2. Again sitting quietly with your eyes closed, reach out and explore your surroundings through touching. Notice textures, shapes, temperatures. As a variation, have someone hand you a series of objects to touch (eg., pencil, apple, cloth, metal, plastic). Discuss your experience with others.
3. Sit looking at an object (eg., book, cup, handbag, shoe). Be aware of all the details of that object: colour, shape, texture. Next look at another person. Do not become involved in a staring contest; merely see what the other person really looks like. Discuss your experience with others.
4. Sitting with your eyes closed have someone pass various scents under your nose (eg., flower, cheese, orange, chocolate, ink). Visualise all of the images that come to mind. Discuss your experience with others.
5. Sitting with your eyes closed have someone place various foods in your mouth. Taste them fully, using your tongue, lips and teeth to experience the food. Discuss your experience with others.

The following diagram, known as the Johari Window (named after the originators, Joe Luft and Harry Ingham), presents a model for learning more about oneself.

FIGURE 2.1 THE JOHARI WINDOW

	Known to Self	**Unknown to Self**
Known to Others	**Free and Open:** You know and others know.	**Blind Self:** You don't know but others do.
Unknown to Others	**Hidden Self:** You know but others do not.	**Unknown Self:** You don't know and others don't know.

Since becoming a counsellor involves increasing self-awareness, the goal should be to make the 'Free and Open' portion larger and the other three areas correspondingly smaller. The process of becoming self-aware and increasing self-understanding involves two important behaviours. First, counsellors must take risks by revealing parts of themselves to others. Secondly, a counsellor must be willing to ask for and receive feedback from others, about how she affects them and how well her behaviour matches her intentions.

Risk-taking involves trying out new behaviours, sharing thoughts and feelings with others and attempting to do those things which might be difficult. In these ways a counsellor begins to discover more about her abilities and limitations, and how people perceive her and react to her.

EXERCISE 2.3

In groups of two or three share information about yourself (ie., self-disclose) by orally completing the following statements:

1. Joining a new group makes me feel . . .
2. I like people to think I am . . .
3. When things are getting me down, I . . .
4. At this moment I feel . . .

5. When I first met you, I thought . . .
6. This exercise . . .

When all of the questions have been completed, discuss what you have just done by answering the following:

1. How did you feel while doing this exercise?
2. Which questions were easiest to answer? Most difficult?
3. Did you use objective and factual information about yourself to answer the questions, or subjective and feeling information? Which is more revealing of yourself? Why?
4. What did you learn about yourself?

This exercise can be made more or less intense or threatening by each person pairing up with, for example, someone they like, dislike, trust, distrust, etc.

Exercise 2.4

To risk doing something new or difficult, think of a situation or activity that you have wanted to change, challenge, confront or attempt, but have never been able to before. For example, you may want to meet a certain stranger, sort out a misunderstanding with a work mate, or volunteer to lead an activity. Think of ways you could accomplish your goal. Choose the one you think is the best and put it into action. Later, discuss the results with others. Why did it succeed? Fail? How do you feel having done it? Was it worth the risk?

Feedback from others provides a counsellor with a valuable source of information. A counsellor must be prepared to learn from more than her own experience so that she can change, modify, and be aware of which of her behaviours are appropriate and which are not.

In giving and receiving feedback counsellors will be most effective if they observe the following guidelines:

1. Give feedback when it is requested. Ask for it only when it is desired.
2. Focus on specific behaviours and avoid sweeping, judgemental statements about a person's character or personality.
3. Use simple, non-technical language when describing another's behaviour.
4. Give feedback on behaviour the other person can control and change.

5. Give feedback as soon after the event or behaviour as possible. Do not store it up for later use.
6. Feedback should be positive as well as negative. People need to know their strengths as well as their weaknesses.
7. Accept the feedback as given, without misconstruing or generalising the specific content.
8. The receiver should have an opportunity to react to the feedback and check its accuracy with others.

EXERCISE 2.5

Seeing yourself as others see you is a powerful method of learning about yourself. There are a number of structured situations that can be used to encourage constructive feedback and sharing of perceptions.

1. Pair up with someone you have had some contact with already.
   Complete the following:
   (a) You seem like the kind of person who . . .
   (b) If you were angry, I would expect you to be . . .
   (c) If you were happy, I would expect you to be . . .
   (d) I appreciate you most when you . . .
   (e) What I like about you right now is . . .
2. Reverse roles with your partner. Speak as though you were your partner. Try to describe yourself as you think your partner sees you. When finished, discuss what happened.

The Counsellor's Personal Qualities

Although there is no clear pattern of personal qualities or characteristics that the effective counsellor must possess, the following are desirable: flexibility, warmth, acceptance of others, open-mindedness, empathy, self-awareness, genuineness, respect for others, non-dominance and objectivity. To state that they are essential is quite another matter. Researching these qualities is complicated by a number of factors such as imprecision of language, problems of control and measurement, and usefulness of the results in other situations. In trying to describe the effective counsellor the best that can be done seems to be to supplement research findings with expert opinion, personal experience, and common sense.

Perhaps a more useful way of indicating the personal qualities desirable in the counsellor would be to describe three areas of counselling in which they are important: the counsellor as a model, the counselling relationship, and the counsellor's courage to counsel.

The counsellor as a model. Modelling takes place in most learning situations. Essentially it is a means of learning through imitating the actions of others. In counselling, clients imitate the counsellor's actions and take certain of her beliefs and attitudes as their own. This process is inevitable and beyond the counsellor's control. A counsellor, however, should be aware of and accepting of herself, her values and behaviours, so that she presents a consistent model for effective relating and problem-solving. Such characteristics as being open, non-biased, non-judgemental, sensitive and caring can then be seen as directly related to effective helping.

The counselling relationship. It is widely accepted by practitioners and theorists that the relationship between counsellor and client is an important aspect of counselling. Effective counsellors are those who can establish caring, non-threatening relationships with their clients in which both feel safe and secure enough to interact as real, spontaneous people. The quality of this relationship can itself be therapeutic and depends very largely on the counsellor being a real person.

The courage to counsel. In order to help others counsellors need courage and self-confidence. There are many times when it would be easier for a counsellor to opt out of helping: to ignore a plea for help; make excuses for not wanting to become involved with another person; or judge a situation to be hopeless, unrealistic, trivial or outside her area of competence. To make a commitment to help another person carries with it responsibilities and uncertainties. Anyone who seriously intends to become an effective counsellor must be willing to accept those responsibilities and uncertainties and place herself in situations of personal, emotional, interpersonal and vocational risk. Again, the counsellor must be prepared to function as a whole and real person rather than as a performer acting only within safely prescribed limits.

Role-playing as a Counselling Skill

Much of living and learning involves the playing of roles. This is particularly true in counselling, both in training to be a counsellor and working therapeutically with clients. Role-playing itself is not a unique or unusual form of behaviour. All relationships involve role-playing, since people relate to others as holders of a certain role, status or position.

Role-playing is the process of acting the part of a real or imagined person. When used in counsellor training, it has a number of potential benefits for counsellors:

1. By role-playing real situations early in training, counsellors can feel free to make mistakes and try new behaviours without worrying about adverse effects on clients.
2. Role-playing enables counsellors to experience what it feels like to be a client and to develop ability and confidence in portraying and expressing feelingsand ideas.
3. Role-playing helps counsellors to learn by doing rather than by merely discussing techniques and strategies in an abstract and intellectual manner.
4. Role-playing is useful in learning about the dynamics of forming and building a relationship.

There are difficulties in role-playing as a training device, however. Many people find it threatening. This threat should be faced and overcome by intending counsellors. Also, some people are so guarded or unimaginative in expressing their feelings that they are ineffective in role-playing, or they portray clients who are difficult to work with, emotionally dull and unresponsive. Those who have this difficulty should practise expressing their own feelings, even exaggerating them, until they are able to express easily and realistically a wide range of emotions. A related problem is that of trying to beat or frustrate the counsellor by playing an impossibly difficult client. The aim of role-playing is not to compete against a counsellor but to simulate a real counselling situation.

Role-playing may be criticised as being artificial. While there is some justification for this view, most role-players report that they very quickly forget about themselves and become totally engrossed in the part they are playing. If individuals persist in labelling the situation as artificial and refuse to take part, they may be avoiding something in themselves and should be asked to evaluate their stance. Role-playing, whether from detailed, scripted material or from wholly imagined material, is ultimately an expression of each player's self, her beliefs, attitudes and feelings. Players become engrossed in their parts because the roles they are playing are really extensions of themselves. Thus, whatever the supposed difficulties of role-playing as a training device, it allows people an opportunity to experience new situations, practise new behaviours, reveal themselves in safety and gain confidence and skill in relating to others.

In counselling, much of what a counsellor asks, encourages, or suggests to a client to do, involves acting differently or changing aspects of his behaviour; in short, playing new or more effective roles. The counsellor should be willing and able to model the behaviours she wants the client to try.

EXERCISE 2.6

1. Group role-playing. Someone from the group plays the role of client while the rest of the group simultaneously play counsellor. The client can role-play any problem, concern or situation he wishes. As the counsellors begin to respond, the client should deal with one response at a time, saying, 'Yes, that would encourage me to continue because . . .', or 'No, that would not encourage me to continue because . . .'. When a 'Yes' response is received from the group, the client should continue as though in a real counselling situation.

   When finished, the client describes what it felt like to be a client, and the exercise is repeated with another person playing the part of client. This method of role-playing minimises the threat to any one person by having several people play counsellor at once. It also gives those playing counsellor some information about how effective their responses are, and at the same time forces the client to be aware of how he feels in that role and in response to what is said to him.

2. The large group divides into smaller groups of three or four. Two people role-play an interview situation as in the first exercise above. Those people not role-playing should act as observers and comment on how authentic the role-play seems and how helpful or otherwise the counsellor's statements seem. Repeat this situation until all the people have played counsellor and client.

3. Finally, people pair up and discuss real situations with their partners. Everyone has something they are concerned about and which they can safely share with another person. The topic does not have to be a major concern or worry, but should be current. The counsellor's aim is to listen, understand and respond as helpfully as she can. After 15 minutes, switch roles and repeat.

   This variation makes the situation more authentic and gives the person playing client the opportunity to experience what it is like to ask for and receive help.

Summary

In this chapter we have emphasised that the counsellor, too, must be a real person. Since much of what happens in counselling depends on the relationship between the counsellor and the client, we consider it essential for anyone intending to be a counsellor to give careful thought to her needs to be a counsellor, to begin developing her self-awareness, and to give consideration to those personal qualities that contribute to effective counselling. Completion of these tasks indicates a readiness to begin training in the specific skills of counselling.

3

Beginning a Counselling Relationship

The first contact between a counsellor and a client often has a significant effect on later contacts. A warm, trusting relationship needs to be built up and continued if change is eventually to take place. The client will look for empathy, respect and sensitivity from the counsellor. She will want to feel that the counsellor has the ability to see a situation as she does, to feel with her and to assume her frame of reference. She will respond to a friendly, caring and considerate manner and to being helped to be specific about her feelings and experiences. These three aspects, empathy, respect and concreteness are among those which facilitate the development of a counselling relationship.

The client may wonder whether she is free to express her real concerns. In effect she sums up the counsellor and the counselling situation while responding. She may consider a series of internal questions such as: Am I welcome? Can I trust this counsellor? Is a relationship possible? Will it be satisfying? Can this counsellor help me?

Answers to such questions will be provided not merely by words. Other, often more subtle and powerful means of communication are the physical setting, the way the client is greeted, the counsellor's gestures and tone of voice, and the presence or absence of distractions. All of these convey messages to the client.

From the outset it is vital that the counsellor be alert to the many factors that influence progress. These include being a good objective observer of the client and of the whole physical and social setting, helping the client to express herself in her own way, and being aware of his own role as a possible stimulus to the client and a model for her to copy.

This chapter will examine the first sighting and meeting, getting started, and active, accurate listening. Because counselling occurs in a reciprocal relationship, the counsellor's awareness of himself will also be considered. This counselling relationship is a dynamic one involving specific behaviours that can be identified and practised.

First Considerations

Is the Client Voluntary or Involuntary?

This question considers whether the client has freely chosen to come, whether she has been persuaded, or whether the counsellor has asked to see her, as may often happen in a school setting.

After the initial greetings it is often helpful to deal with this issue straight away. A voluntary client may be easier to work with initially because a decision has already been made to seek help. This implies at least some recognition of a problem and some desire to change. Sometimes, however, it may mask a desire to use the counsellor in a manipulative way.

In some settings some clients perceive the counsellor as someone who can be used to ease pressures that are legitimately exerted by other people. As soon as the counsellor senses that this may be occurring, he should test this hunch, if necessary by confrontation. Coyness, guile, and game-playing on the part of the client should not be paid back in kind. The counsellor's model of open and direct expression of feelings and perceptions is the best counter to clients' attempts to 'con' him.

Another example of an attempt at manipulation is the attempt to put the counsellor 'down'. This may take the form of questioning or scoffing at his experience, methods and qualifications. If the client should object on a point that is valid and relevant to the discussion, the counsellor should simply acknowledge this and then move back to the discussion as smoothly as possible. Counsellors who feel defensive about such matters and attempt to debate or deny the point or to justify themselves, will usually make an awkward situation worse. It is probably best to say calmly, 'I don't think that's relevant here.'

With an involuntary client our experience suggests that it can be very productive to deal immediately with the client's reactions to being present.

The counsellor may:

1. State who referred the client.
2. Give the reason for the referral, eg., 'Mr James is concerned because you have

been very quiet in class lately and the standard of your work has slipped.'

3. Tell the client what might be offered by a counsellor.
4. Invite the client to express feelings about being in this situation. Is she angry? afraid? puzzled? uncertain?
5. Emphasise that the client is free to remain or leave. Often, acceptance of the freedom to leave without being pursued is the first step in establishing the trust which will lead to the client's voluntary return.
6. Suggest that while the client may reject you as her helper there are other sources of help for her problem. Name these sources if the client is interested.

In some instances clients may continue to be reluctant or reticent about participating in counselling. Techniques for engaging these clients are discussed more fully on page 46.

What Background Information is Available and How Much is Needed?

The answers to this question will be determined by the counselling setting, the nature and extent of the problem, the purpose of the counselling, the relevance of background information, the preferences of the counsellor, and the availability of the information.

The setting. Detailed information may be more pertinent in the clinical setting of a psychiatric unit where long-term, in-depth counselling is to take place than in, for example, a Citizen's Advice Bureau where the contact may be limited to one visit.

The nature and extent of the problem. Comprehensive, detailed background information may be desirable if major personality change is sought but is unnecessary if the problem is one of learning certain skills such as how to be more assertive or how to conduct oneself during a job interview.

Purpose of counselling. If a person wishes to free herself from patterns of emotional reaction and behaviour that have their roots in her upbringing it can be pertinent to know something of the family dynamics. However, if the client seeks information on job requirements, legal rights, or child development, background information on the client may not be essential or even relevant.

Relevance. Information about educational qualifications would be relevant in vocational counselling but probably not in marriage guidance. A social worker engaged in a welfare inquiry would be vitally interested in details of family income but this would be irrelevant to a school counsellor dealing with a conflict between peers.

The Counsellor's Preferences

1. A counsellor may prefer to gain his impressions of the client and his analysis of the problem from first-hand contact rather than be influenced by background information. He may want to leave his mind free from preconceptions or from the interpretations of other people.
2. A counsellor may prefer to obtain background information incidentally during the course of an interview.
3. A counsellor may prefer to obtain background information before first meeting the client, in the interests of greater understanding of the client, economy of time or as a guide to leading in the interview.
4. A counsellor may prefer to obtain information in a structured interview as a way of beginning a relationship.

Availability of Information

In some settings, such as schools and medical centres, comprehensive records are available to be consulted by workers within that setting. The information may also be available to social workers, psychologists and others with a professional interest in the client. In other settings and circumstances information may not be divulged in order to preserve confidentiality. Sometimes information may be offered directly by the client, or she may give permission for it to be obtained elsewhere. The credibility of the source of background information is an aspect to be considered.

Types of Information

It is unlikely that a voluntary rather than a professional counsellor would need information on all the following topics but these are the areas generally included in a comprehensive case history or case study.

Name	**Address**	**Race**
Dates of Contacts	**Date of Birth**	**Place of Birth**

Problem. (Nature, onset, seriousness, duration, previous attempts to deal with it. Opinions and attitudes of others, eg., parents, teachers, employers, medical personnel.)

Family. (Names, ages, occupations and sex of family members, socio-economic status, cultural patterns, family relationships, health problems, religion.)

Physical Health. (Hearing, eyesight, serious illnesses, current health, appearance.)

Psychological Test Results.

Educational History and Achievements.

Social Development. (Sociability and adaptability, friends, participation in groups.)

Emotional Development. (General mental health, stability, self-image, predominant moods, signs of stress eg. tics, twitching, tears, stuttering, tantrums.)

Work Experience. (Place and dates of employment. Type of work performed. Attitude towards work. Vocational plans and aspirations.)

General Summing-Up.

The First Sighting and Meeting

The client and counsellor immediately begin sizing up each other. Each begins a process of observing and silently questioning. An internal dialogue such as that in column 2 of Figure 3.1 may take place in the counsellor's mind.

The counsellor should be aware of the following:

1. *Client's physical appearance*
   Would it create problems for the client?
   Does it give a clue about health? about self-image? (eg., the tidiness of clothing, personal hygiene.)
2. *Manner and bearing*
   Does the client appear nervous? withdrawn? aggressive? defensive? passive?
3. *Movement and gestures*
   Is the client still or moving about?
   What is she doing with her hands? her head? her feet?
   What is the possible meaning of her movements and gestures?
4. *Posture and stance*
   Is the client upright? hunched over? standing freely? supporting herself on furniture? What does this mean?
5. *Surroundings*
   Is the counselling setting private? relatively informal?

Is the decor of the room warm and relaxing?
Is there freedom from extraneous noise?
Are the seats comfortable? well-placed?
Is the counsellor behind a desk? beside it? in front of it?

6. *Differences in social status*
   Does the client's clothing indicate poverty? wealth? social position? state of mind?
7. *Physical distance*
   Is the client so close to you as to be threatened by the closeness?
   Are the counsellor and client comfortably apart?
8. *Eye contact*
   Is the client able to look you in the eye or does she avoid your gaze?

Self-awareness

Counselling occurs in a reciprocal relationship. The client, as well as the counsellor, is observing and reacting (see column 3 of Figure 3.1). Success in counselling depends considerably upon the client's perceptions of the counsellor's manner and behaviour. The client will be aware of and react to the counsellor's eye contact, posture, gesture and manner. She will react to the length and delay of the counsellor's responses, interruptions, amount of talk and voice quality.

Good eye contact involves looking at the client when she is talking and using glances that express interest and acceptance. A piercing stare, look of blankness, or avoidance of the client's gaze will be disconcerting to her. People tend to use eye contact more when listening than when speaking.

The counsellor should sit facing the client in an open, relaxed manner, and far enough away from her to feel comfortable. His hands should be kept relatively still and his facial expressions friendly.

FIGURE 3.1 A POSSIBLE INTERNAL DIALOGUE ON FIRST MEETING

Attribute	Counsellor Observations and Questions	Client Observations and Questions
Physical Appearance	She is very thin and pale . . . Is she ill? under strain? depressed? Her hair is untidy and her blouse has a button missing . . . Is she depressed?	He's so big and tall . . . reminds me of my father. It's frightening. Can I trust him?
Manner	She is withdrawn. Is she depressed? reluctant to be here?	His voice is warm and friendly. He looks me in the eye and smiles.
Bearing	She is hunched over, holding herself tightly. Is she afraid of me? of the situation? of revealing her anxiety?	He looks relaxed and calm. He is upright but not stiff. His hands are at his side. He seems at ease. Can I relax too?
Movement and Gestures	She is turning her head away from me, twisting her hands, moving her left foot up and down. She twitches. Is she very tense and anxious?	He is fairly still but not stiff and tense.
Posture	She is sitting hunched up on the edge of the chair. Is she very tense? defensive?	He is leaning slightly towards me. His hands are loosely clasped.
Stance	She is turned away from me, presenting her shoulder, not her face.	He is seated to the side of me, facing me. I don't feel as if I am being confronted.
Surroundings	I've told the secretary not to put any phone calls through for half-an-hour. Hope she remembers. It's a bit cold . . . Should I turn on the heater?	It's private in here. I like the gold curtains. This chair is comfortable. Can I relax now? Maybe?
Eye Contact	She can't look me in the eye consistently. She darts quick glances at me now and then.	His eyes look warm. I want to look at him but I can't manage to keep looking at him yet. I think I can trust him.

Slouching, playing with a pen, frowning or too much movement are distracting.

Getting the client to talk freely is important in the initial stages. A warm, pleasant tone of voice, simple language and medium volume make the counsellor's conversation more effective. A counsellor who talks too much discourages the client who may well feel that her ideas are not important. If the counsellor can delay responses naturally, there is an increased chance that the client will talk and explain more. Short counsellor responses also encourage this, as does a minimum of interruption. The client can feel that she is accepted, worthwhile, and free to speak.

The following exercises are designed to allow the participants to experience the effects of various physical surroundings, gestures, eye contact, and other attributes, as discussed above. (Leaders may find it valuable to have course members do the exercises before reading those sections.) The exercises may be done as demonstrations before a large group or they may be done in small groups with one participant taking the part of the counsellor, another the client, and the others acting as observers.

EXERCISE 3.1*

Client Reactions

After each exercise the client should share her reactions to what happened. She may share with the whole group or with her small group only.

1. Physical Conditions
   (a) Experiment with three chair positions.

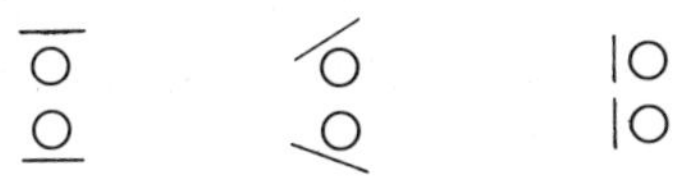

   In which situation did the client feel most comfortable?

   (b) Vary the counsellor's position in relation to a desk.

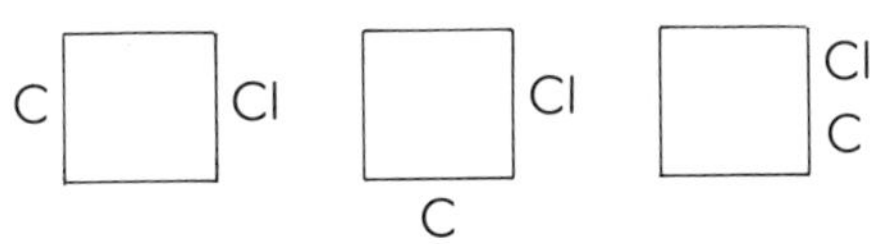

   In what way did the client feel differently towards the counsellor's being in each of these positions in relation to the desk?

2. Eye Contact
   (a) Counsellor looks at ceiling, out the window, at the bookshelf, anywhere but directly at the client.
   (b) Counsellor makes eye contact with the client without staring her out.
3. Movement, Gesture, Posture, Stance
   (a) Counsellor sits upright at his desk, plays with a pencil, bends a paperclip, taps his foot against the desk.
   (b) Counsellor leans against the wall and waves his arms around while talking.
   (c) Counsellor leans forward towards the client while already sitting close with his knees almost touching hers.
   (d) Counsellor sits on his chair in a relaxed way, hands held loosely, and leans forward slightly.
4. Greeting
   (a) Counsellor with his tie askew and hair ruffled is looking in the filing cabinet. Greets client with 'Just a minute will you.' Continues to search the files, takes out a folder, slams the drawer shut, produces a comb, combs his hair, straightens his tie and at last says 'What did you say your name was again?'
   (b) Replay in a more welcoming manner.

EXERCISE 3.2*

Counsellor Reactions

Ask a counsellor what the client might be experiencing.

1. Client sits perched on the edge of the chair, twisting her hands and staring at the floor.
2. Client sits upright, holding herself tightly, hands clasped firmly and launches into a complaint in self-righteous tones.
3. Client sits down and bursts into tears.
4. Client refuses to speak.

EXERCISE 3.3

Self-awareness

1. Eye Contact
   (a) Form pairs. Stand 1-2 metres away from your partner. One partner at a

time looks at the eyes of the other and then says what the other is looking at.

(b) Each in turn looks at his partner's forehead, nose, chin, neck, and shoulders in that sequence. See when your partner can tell you are *not* looking into his eyes.

(c) Maintain eye contact with your partner while paying him a compliment and receiving his response. Repeat while criticism is offered. (If you do not know your partner you may have to confine your compliment or criticism to outward appearance or clothing.)

2. Voice Quality
   (a) Form pairs. Make the statement, 'Hullo, Paul. I'm pleased you could come', in two ways:
   (i) In a flat, uninterested way.
   (ii) In a warm, welcoming way.
   Listen carefully to the difference and invite your partner to react.
   (b) Carry on your conversation from the above opening statement. Get your partner to comment on the quality of your voice.

3. Counsellor Responses
   (a) A training course leader should make a tape of a segment of conversation demonstrating effective and ineffective use of timing and length of responses and interruptions. Group members should be invited to comment.
   (b) Alternatively, such a segment of conversation could be role-played to the group.

Getting Started

Open Invitation to Talk

If the client is invited to talk freely, instead of being subjected to a series of questions, she is more likely to present her problem. In part the invitation to speak will be conveyed by the counsellor's posture, manner, gesture and tone of voice. The words used will make the message explicit.

After the client has been received into the room, greeted and seated, a statement can be made, or a question asked, that tells her that she is welcome and recognised, and that it is her right to define the problem. It also says that the counsellor is ready to listen and help.

For example:

'How can I help you?'

'Tell me what is bothering you.'

'My secretary said that when you phoned you were concerned about . . .'

'What's on your mind?'

The counsellor should use a warm, accepting tone and words that are natural to him. He should avoid stereotyping beginning statements or using false humour. He should also be wary of imputing 'worry' or 'problems' unless the client has already used such terms. Occasionally counsellors are faced with clients who are initially resistant or reluctant to participate in counselling. Techniques for engaging these clients are discussed on page 46.

Exercise 3.4*

In pairs, alternating the role of counsellor and client, give open invitations to speak to the following:

(a) A distraught mother whose teenage son is disrupting family life.
(b) A middle-aged man just made redundant.
(c) A teenage girl with a career inquiry.

Discuss the effectiveness of your statements.

Sorting Issues

Some clients may respond to the counsellor's open invitation to talk with a torrent of problems or concerns. They may talk non-stop for several minutes and describe a number of related or unrelated problems. Since it is necessary for both the client and counsellor to fully understand and clarify the client's concerns, the counsellor can begin by responding in a way that will help the client sort the issues. This is done by simply listing the concerns the client has mentioned and inviting her to select the one that she thinks should be dealt with first. For example:

Client: I've had it with school! The work is too hard; the English teacher picks on me; Mum and Dad nag me about not having enough homework to do; and two of my best friends have been ignoring me lately.

Counsellor: You have mentioned several things: the difficulty of the work; the English teacher's attitude toward you; your parents' concerns about your lack of homework; and problems with two of your friends. Which of these do you want to talk about first?

The skill of sorting issues indicates that the counsellor has been listening, is actively concerned, and is willing to focus on issues the client thinks are most pressing.

Exercise 3.5

In pairs, alternating the role of counsellor and client, use the skill of sorting issues in response to the following:

1. 'Nothing is going right. I hate work; can't stand the sight of the place. And when I get home, the kids jump on me with a whole day's demands and problems. I never get any help from anyone – always have to do everything myself.'
2. 'Well, let's see. I guess it's really my own lack of self-confidence. I mean, I suppose I should know how to do those things, but I don't. Where would I even go to learn? And my parents don't really help things. They just criticise me for being lazy. What can I say to them? What do I do?'
3. 'I'm trying to decide what subjects to take next year. I would really like to do more art, but Dad says that I need all the science I can get. Since I won't be going to university, is there any use in taking physics and chemistry? I don't really like them and can't see me ever using any of it. And that's another problem. What work will I be able to do if I don't pass my exams?'

Open-ended Questions

Open-ended questions or statements invite the client to continue talking by suggesting that she give more details about a topic she has introduced.

For example:

'What is it about your mother that frustrates you so much?'

In contrast, closed questions tend to shut off conversation by inviting a 'Yes' or 'No' answer. A series of such questions or statements can sound like an interrogation.

For example:

'It sounds as if your mother frustrates you.'

'Yes.'

'Does she make you angry too?'

'Yes.'

'You'd like to get away from her?'

'Not really.'

'Oh, I thought you'd want to leave home.'

'No.'

Open-ended questions are important particularly in the early stages of an interview. Beginning questions with: what? when? how? where? why? is one useful way of making them open.

Open-ended statements or questions give the counsellor clues or free information to follow up and thus keep the conversation going. They also indicate to the client that she is free to lead the dialogue where she wants.

Exercise 3.6*

1. Which of the following are open-ended?
   (a) Do you like peanuts?
   (b) Why did you return to school this year?
   (c) How would you get rid of such a nuisance?
   (d) Is it time to go home?
2. Rewrite the following as open-ended questions.
   (a) Did you enjoy the party?
   (b) Did you leave school because you wanted to earn money?
   (c) Have we got enough money to get home?
   (d) Did you get that jacket at a sale?

Topic Following

Topic following means focusing on what the client has actually said rather than taking the topic in a new direction or adding to its meaning.

For example:

'I see what you mean.'

'Tell me more about it.'

It is used in the early stages of a contact when a client pauses. In a warm attentive way, the counsellor, with a short statement or question, helps the client to go on exploring the topic to make her aware that he is really listening to her.

Exercise 3.7*

Add a statement or question to each of the following client statements so that the topic is followed. You may write the statements, say them in pairs and, if desired, tape the dialogues.

1. 'I can't seem to get a job. Whenever I go for an interview they say they'll get in touch but they never do.'
2. 'My mother insists that I get home by 12 pm whenever I'm out. Sometimes that's just impossible.'
3. 'I hate school! The teachers, the rules, the uniform, the lot!'

Minimal Encouragers

Minimal encouragers are gestures, nods, single words or noises, body postures or repetitions of key words that indicate that the counsellor is interested and involved, but that the client is in control of deciding which way the interview will go. They should be used early in the contact within the natural flow of the dialogue. Examples include:

'Mmm'

'A-ha'

'Yes?'

'So?'

'Your mother?'

Minimal encouragers are effective in keeping the client talking, whereas too much talk from the counsellor may lose the client. She may easily get the message, 'This is not my interview. He wants to hear his own voice, not mine.'

Exercise 3.8

Practise using minimal encouragers in conversations you have at home, or at work or in counselling situations. Share any comments you may have about their use with others in your training course. Note the use of minimal encouragers while watching a TV programme.

Active, Accurate Listening

Listening is basic to all interviews. It requires that the counsellor be silent most of the time and use all his senses to get the total message. He listens with his ears to the words spoken and the tone of voice, with his mind to the underlying message, and with his eyes to the language of the body in its posture, bearing and gestures. The counsellor also listens to himself: he notes his reactions to the message he is receiving and to the way he is coping with it. A number of specific listening skills will be covered in chapter 4.

Active, accurate listening is vital throughout an interview but especially at the beginning when the counsellor usually takes a less verbally active part. The counsellor listens by tuning in with his being to the other person, concentrating on her, allowing her messages to be paramount. This is intended to communicate *empathy* ie., to prove that the counsellor *heard, understood* and *accepted* what has been said to him.

Exercise 3.9

1. Two group members have a conversation on an agreed topic where some personal feeling would be expressed. This takes 3 to 4 minutes.
2. One observer listens mainly to the client's words and summarises the message.
3. Another observer concentrates on the body language of the client.
4. The rest of the group can listen to the total message but also be especially aware of their own reactions to the client's statements.

Thinking Aloud

Occasionally a client says something that leads the counsellor to believe that a shift in topic could be productive. Rather than making a seemingly abrupt change which may leave the client puzzled or irritated, the counsellor should think aloud.

For example:

During a vocational interview a client interested in medical laboratory work for which there are limited vacancies, reveals that her school subjects are English, mathematics, physics, chemistry and biology. The counsellor may then inquire whether the client has ever considered careers in commerce. Lest this switch seem inexplicable, the counsellor could think aloud, something like this:

'There are limited vacancies in medical laboratory work. I wonder whether you have ever considered careers in commerce. It is possible to take these up without having studied commercial subjects at school. Your maths is strong and could be used in accounting or data processing.'

Immediacy

Immediacy is recognising what is going on between the counsellor and the client at a particular moment and communicating this constructively. Because this communication usually refers to feelings, it can be very powerful, and it may be threatening to a client who is unused to intimate, honest communication. Therefore, it should be done tentatively and expressed only as an opinion. It indicates that the counsellor accepts the person sufficiently to be completely open about their interaction.

For example:

'I'm feeling that maybe you are becoming irritated with me right now.'

'I feel that perhaps you're reluctant to be here.'

The Use of Silence

We are often afraid of, or embarrassed by, silences during conversations. Silences, however, may be as revealing as the spoken word. Acceptance of a client's silence may emphasise to her that it is her right to determine the nature of the interview. It allows both counsellor and client time to think. It builds trust and may eventually encourage the client to be very frank in her revelations.

To use silence effectively the counsellor needs to accept its worth, to feel confident about allowing it to continue, and to be sensitive to timing. If possible, the counsellor should let the client be the first to break the silence. If, however, the silence seems to convey a strong sense of resentment on the part of the client, especially an involuntary one, it can be helpful to verbalise this and invite the client to leave if she wishes.

EXERCISE 3.10

1. When replaying a video or audio-tape of one of your interviews, note whenever: a new topic was introduced, you thought aloud, you used immediacy, you used silence.
   (a) Note what happened immediately before your use of each skill.
   (b) Note the effect of using each skill.
2. Alternatively, during role-playing or actual interviews, an observer could be asked to note these things for you.

Engaging Reluctant Clients

This section has been adapted from an article by R.J. Manthei and D.A. Matthews. Reluctant or resistant clients are part of every counsellor's experience. Faced with reluctant clients, counsellors can choose to accept their reluctance at face value, i.e. as an unequivocal refusal of help. Alternatively, they can sensitively and non-judgementally attempt to engage the client so that the real meaning of the reluctance may become clear. Many reluctant clients may need only to find genuineness, reassurance, and the right invitation from a counsellor to begin a relationship. When working with such clients, it is essential to allow them time to feel comfortable and develop trust, to refrain from pre-judging clients' moods, motives, and needs, and to try out more than the normal variety of invitations to talk or participate.

INTERPRETING THE CLIENT'S SILENCE

Initially, confronted with a client's silence, the counsellor should try to assess what the silence means for the client, and some of the reasons for the behaviour.

Silence can express many things: anger, fear, boredom, respect, embarrassment, sadness, contempt. Counsellors should make every attempt to understand the possible meanings of silence. In doing this, particular attention should be paid to the client's movements, gestures and physical appearance. Commenting on these things can result in the client agreeing with or correcting the observation. Either way, the client has been engaged.

Interpreting clients' feelings can be accomplished by written means. For example, clients may respond to a written observation or a simple drawing. When using written messages, counsellors should write simply and briefly, in large letters and in full view of the client.

Mirroring as a form of interpretation can be used to highlight dominant aspects of a client's behaviour. In this technique, counsellors imitate movements, gestures, or postures that seem meaningful. Mirroring can be a provocative form of interpretation and may elicit a strong response, positive or negative.

Encouraging Non-Verbal Responding

These techniques are intended to encourage the client to initiate exploration and self-disclosure without having to verbalise thoughts and feelings.

It is often effective to invite clients to draw or write thoughts or feelings they find hard to verbalise.

Clients can be encouraged to express thoughts physically: eg. by acting, miming, or posturing. Almost any verbal message can be communicated physically in a way that makes the meaning more clear and direct.

Having once engaged clients to act out thoughts or feelings, counsellors should ask them to exaggerate specific behaviours. Repeating a gesture with emphasised movement may aid a client to clarify its meaning and the personal feelings that lie behind it.

Working at the Client's Pace

Many counsellors, pressed by time and institutional demands, quickly become frustrated with reluctant clients. In some cases dealing with the reluctance indirectly will foster trust and the development of an appropriate relationship.

Counsellors should try taking reluctant clients for a walk; giving them some small non-counselling task to do; allowing them to remain while the counsellor continues with other work. The client may simply need time to get to know and trust the counsellor enough to begin talking.

Clients can be asked to bring photographs of self, family or friends, that they are willing to share. Some of the techniques described earlier can then be used to comment on and interpret the photograph.

If clients are agreeable, they can be given some small bit of 'homework' to perform before the next session. They may be curious, and co-operate long enough to see what the counsellor has in mind.

The counsellor can try changing seating positions and/or activities. In some cases a mere change of position or activity will result in a client being more willing to interact.

Responding to the Talkative Reluctant Client

Some reluctant clients will readily verbalise feelings such as hostility and anger, or interact in over-compliant or evasive ways. The effect is the same: avoidance of meaningful contact with the counsellor.

As in the case of the silent client, counsellors should pay particular attention to the talkative client's movements, gestures and physical appearance.

The manner in which a client speaks may reveal as much as what is actually said. Counsellors should be sensitive to voice quality and use such information in responding.

In many instances it will be productive to have clients repeat particular statements, phrases, or words. This repetition can serve to highlight underlying feelings and to clarify meanings.

Counsellors should notice clients' use of language. For example, when clients use 'need' when what is really meant is 'want'. 'Need' may imply helplessness, while 'want' implies autonomy and the ability to change. Similar attention can be given to the differences between 'you' and 'I', 'we' and 'me', 'can't' and 'won't', the 'passive' voice and the 'active' voice.

If video-tape equipment is available, clients can be asked to view themselves and comment on what they see.

Explaining the Counselling Process

In some cases, clients' reluctance to engage in counselling can be largely overcome by explaining the counselling process, how it works, and what the client can expect from the counsellor. The mere fact that counsellors are prepared to reveal their motives, intentions, thoughts and feelings can act as an incentive and model for the client to do likewise.

These suggestions indicate the range of counsellor behaviours that could be used if the reluctant or difficult client is approached with patience, open-mindedness, sensitivity and creativity.

Counsellors should be aware of the possibility that generally co-operative clients may show reluctance when certain topics are introduced. Counsellors should also remember that they do not have the right to persist in efforts to engage unwilling clients to talk. Reluctance may show something more than a temporary reticence. It may indicate a message that should be heeded: Leave me alone. In the face of marked resistance the counsellor should try referring the client elsewhere or simply end the contact. The counsellor should regard these as appropriate moves and not necessarily as signs of personal failure.

REVIEW EXERCISE 3.11

In order to review the skills in this chapter and to make sure they are understood and can be put to use, make two or three lists of five different skills each. Then, role-play an interview with another person and try to use each of the skills listed. It should be possible to use each of the five skills in a five minute interview. Ask an observer to check that each skill has been used. Repeat using other lists of skills.

Summary

First impressions count. If a counsellor can convey warmth, acceptance and empathy to a client through a welcoming setting, an appropriate voice and gestures, and the use of skills such as active, accurate listening, a facilitative relationship can begin. This sets the scene for the analysis of problems and subsequent action to produce change.

4

Developing a Counselling Relationship

The second stage of helping involves (a) maintaining the good working relationship developed in the first stage and (b) taking the process further by helping the client explore, clarify and define his problem or area of concern. The skills that are most appropriate and effective at this stage are those which enable the client to extend and develop his awareness and understanding of himself and his problem. These skills can be used effectively at any stage of the counselling process. The distinction between skills used to begin a relationship and these skills is not hard and fast and the order of their presentation does not represent any preference.

There are two main divisions of this middle stage of counselling: responding and leading. The counsellor's ability to respond effectively depends on her being able to follow leads the client presents, and to enable the client to think more clearly and understand more accurately. Leading skills become increasingly important in encouraging new ideas, perspectives, and understandings. They differ from responding skills in that the counsellor leads or directs the client's focus of attention in a direction the counsellor has decided is important. When taking an active leading role, the counsellor risks confusing or alienating the client but this risk is reduced by (a) the mutual trust and respect that exists and (b) by the counsellor presenting her leading statements in a tentative manner that allows the client an opportunity to reject or modify them.

Consider these counsellor statements:

1. 'You have said nothing about your father. It is obvious that you fear him.'
2. 'You have said nothing about your father. Is it because you're afraid of him?'

Note the difference. The first is said in a final, judgemental way. It allows the client no opportunity to disagree without directly opposing the counsellor. The second statement is offered tentatively. It allows the client the chance to disagree or offer a modified version without challenging the counsellor.

It is extremely important that the counsellor uses leading responses with caution – only after a sound working relationship has been developed and then in a non-accusing, tentative way.

Responding Skills

These skills reinforce the idea that it is the client who determines the content and direction of the interview. Their use demonstrates counsellor interest in the client and a desire to understand fully what the client is experiencing. Some counsellors may stop using them early in the counselling process because they seem ineffectual or give the impression that the counsellor does not know what to do. However, the counsellor should resist urges to take over and should continue using responding skills until both she and the client are clear about what an idea, feeling or situation really involves. These skills are often difficult to learn because social training discourages people from showing direct interest in other people's feelings for fear of appearing nosey, pushy or even ignorant. In practice, the intimacy of these behaviours is usually welcomed and appreciated by others, especially those who are experiencing some confusion, difficulty or loneliness.

Responding skills are extremely productive in counselling, and beginning counsellors should not be concerned about over-using them.

Feeling Identification

The ability to perceive and respond accurately to another person's feelings is essential if the counsellor is to help that person talk about what is on his mind or underlying his difficulties. Counsellors must be sensitive to more than just the content of a client's message. Very often the way in which the client speaks is more important than the words he uses to express himself.

Responding to feeling is a powerful technique because of its intimacy and the fact that, more than most other counsellor behaviours, it communicates acceptance of and empathy with the client. In normal social interactions, feelings are regularly disguised and controlled. Thus, when someone perceives our feelings accurately, it tends to have a profound effect on us. We usually react positively to the person who has understood us, and we realise that our feelings, whatever they might be, are justified.

Read the following:

Client: I've had it! She always does that to me and I hate it!
Counsellor: Could it be that you're partly to blame?

Client: I've had it! She always does that to me and I hate it!
Counsellor: You really seem angry about this.

Note the difference in the responses. The first deals only with the content of what was said and asks an emotional person to look at his situation rationally. The second recognises the person's feeling state and implies that the feeling is acceptable and has been understood. Think of a similar situation you have been in. What is the effect on you when someone accepts what you have said – words, feeling and all?

The first requirement for dealing with feelings in a counselling situation is to be able to recognise when feelings are being communicated. The counsellor should encourage the client to specify and identify what he feels; she should not rely solely on her own interpretation of what the client might be feeling, no matter how obvious the feeling might appear to be. The counsellor can simply and effectively clarify this by asking some variation of the following:

'How does that make you feel?

'What are you feeling right now?'

Exercise 4.1*

This exercise, adapted from one by John L. Wallen and D.W. Johnson, is designed to highlight the difference between statements that describe exactly how the speaker feels and those that are merely emotional without describing the specific feeling involved.

For each of the following items there are three statements. Only one actually describes a feeling; the others may *contain* or *imply* feeling but do not specifically *describe* the feeling involved. Select the statement that most directly *describes* the speaker's feeling.

1. (a) 'I feel you are always picking on me.'
   (b) 'Leave me alone!'
   (c) 'It angers me when you always blame me.'

2. (a) 'I began to feel depressed when Jill and I broke up. After that nothing seemed to go right.'
   (b) 'I feel things haven't been going right lately, ever since Jill and I broke up.'
   (c) 'Anyone would feel less than his best if he had just lost his girlfriend.'
3. (a) 'My reaction to that assignment was pretty definite.'
   (b) 'Would you like it if you had to do all that work?'
   (c) 'It's not fair that we have to do this. I'm pretty mad about it.'
4. (a) 'I'm afraid about what you've stirred up by talking to my parents.'
   (b) 'I feel that you have really ruined things for me.'
   (c) 'Why did you have to tell my parents? Anybody should know better than to do that.'
5. (a) 'I feel you know a lot about things. I wish I could say that about myself.'
   (b) 'You interest me.'
   (c) 'When you talk, I feel relieved because I know I'm not the only person who feels this way.'
6. (a) 'This is an interesting exercise.'
   (b) 'I really feel challenged by this exercise.'
   (c) 'I'm sure everyone liked doing this exercise.'

Self-expression of Feeling

The measure of a counsellor's success in working with feelings in a counselling situation is largely determined by her ability to recognise her own feelings as they occur and to use them in a manner that is most helpful to the client. Using feelings effectively can mean a number of things. When the counsellor openly shares her feelings with a client, she may be modelling desirable behaviour or enhancing a climate of trust and honesty. Similarly, open expression of feelings can relieve interpersonal tensions and demonstrate to clients that feelings themselves need not be overwhelming or disabling. Even when not directly communicated to the client, the counsellor's feelings can be used constructively. For example, once the counsellor recognises a feeling within herself, she should next determine whether it is the direct result of her interaction with the client or whether it arises out of her own personal experience. In both instances the counsellor can make constructive use of her feelings beyond merely expressing them to the client. The counsellor responses below illustrate this.

1. 'I feel good when you say that. I appreciate being told when I have been helpful.'
2. 'No, I'm not happy to talk to you either. But, now that we're both here, what are we going to do?'
3. 'I'm feeling annoyed by your constant apologies for things. I wonder if others might have the same reaction?'
4. (Thinking to herself): 'I'm nervous. Why? I'm never comfortable when sitting this close to another person.' (To client): 'I'm going to move back slightly so I can be a bit more relaxed.'

In the first response the counsellor is demonstrating how to receive a compliment by simply accepting it without modifying or discounting it. The second response models and enhances interpersonal honesty (the counsellor does not pretend she is glad to see this reluctant client) and may relieve tension by openly sharing negative feelings. In the third response the counsellor expresses a negative reaction to her client but does so in a way that encourages the client to take a closer look at how he may affect others. The counsellor's nervousness in the fourth response arises out of her own experience, but by simply stating what she is going to do and why, her action becomes constructive in the sense that it models direct, open communication.

Feelings should be dealt with as they arise in counselling. The counsellor should be continually aware of how she is feeling and what has caused these feelings. Likewise, the client should be continually encouraged to express and explore his feelings. If feelings remain unspoken, they may dominate the relationship and inhibit a more rational approach to a problem. Often merely recognising and expressing a feeling is enough to lessen it, control it, accept it, or shift one's attention from it.

Think of a situation in which you were very angry. Of the following, which would you prefer to have said to you? Why?

1. 'You know, this whole thing might not be as bad as you think.'
2. 'This whole business has really made you mad!'

Exercise 4.2

1. Take part in a role-play using short client statements that are designed to

provoke some feeling in the counsellor. The following client statements are given as examples:

(a) 'You never say anything! You just sit there nodding and saying "yes" all the time. I thought you were going to help me!'
(b) 'You're so easy to talk to. You seem to understand everything I say and do. I just know you will do something for me.'
(c) 'You lied. You said that what we talked about here was just between us, but this morning the teacher asked me if I had talked to you yet. You had no right to tell him I was coming.'
(d) 'What's the matter with you? I've said I don't know but you don't seem to believe me. If I knew what to do, I wouldn't be here.'
(e) 'Leave me alone. (Long silence) . . .'

The counsellor role-player should respond to each client statement by identifying her own feeling reaction to the client. For example, the counsellor may feel hurt or guilty or even angry in response to client statement (a) above.

2. When the counsellor is quickly and accurately able to recognise the feelings within herself, she should write a constructive response and then discuss it with the client role-player to determine its effect. The counsellor may write something like the following in response to statement (a) above: 'You're mad and confused about what I'm doing. How would you like me to act?'

3. Finally, individuals make up client statements of their own. Teachers, counsellors, social workers and probation officers can use situations that are typical of their own work. The statements can be audio or videotaped if such equipment is available. This allows the same material to be used on several occasions.

Exercise 4.3

As you do the exercises in this book, note your feelings and reactions. As often as possible stop working, identify your feeling and express it either in writing or orally. For example, you may feel foolish or irritated, excited or pleased. Write or say what you feel, such as: 'I feel nervous about role-playing in front of a group.' By doing this you will become more aware of your present feelings and will be able to express them more accurately and quickly.

Reflection

Effective use of reflection conveys to the client that the counsellor is trying to understand what he has said, that she has understood correctly and that she accepts him. A counsellor can reflect content by a short, simple re-statement or paraphrasing of the essence of what the client has actually said. Reflection of content condenses and crystallises in a fresh way the information a client gives. The counsellor can also reflect feeling, that part of the client's statement that represents the emotional message. Often what is said (content) does not communicate the real meaning. Reflection of feeling focuses on this underlying or unstated message.

Reflection should be used to demonstrate understanding, but more importantly, to facilitate the client's movement toward more complete self-awareness and self-understanding. It is appropriate and effective to use reflection skills at any stage of the counselling process.

For example:

Client: I don't think I could do it. I'd only fail. I . . . well – I've never been able to get grades like that before and I'm sure I couldn't now.

Counsellor: (content reflection) Your past records convince you it's not possible now.

(feeling reflection) You're feeling a bit afraid to even try.

EXERCISE 4.4

In the following exercise there are four client statements. After each one write (a) the counsellor response that best reflects the content of the statement, and (b) the response that best reflects feeling ie., the response which indicates that you understand the client's attitude and the situation as it appears to him.

Compare and discuss your answers with others doing the same exercise.

1. 'No, I won't! I'm not going to tell you any of my business. I didn't ask to see you. I was sent! You're not getting anything out of me!'
2. 'I really need your help. I just can't seem to make friends with any decent kids. They just ignore me and – I don't know – I just feel – I'm wondering is there something wrong with me? Do *you* think there's something wrong with me?'
3. 'Nearly two more years! Honestly I just couldn't stand two more years of school. Oh, I can do it all right – I know I can pass the exams. But it's all so boring! I'm changing my mind about going to university.'
4. 'Well, OK, it *is* at home. But what difference does it make talking to you about

it? You wouldn't understand. You just don't know what it's like there day after day.'

Exercise 4.5

Next time you are listening to an interview on a television or radio current events programme, notice how often the interviewer reflects the *feeling* of the person being interviewed as opposed to the *content* of what has been said. What seems to be the effect of each type of reflection on the person interviewed?

Accurate Understanding

In counselling it is necessary to understand what the client is saying and to be able to communicate your understanding to him. Understanding involves far more than merely hearing the words that are spoken. It necessitates careful listening to, and awareness of, all the verbal and non-verbal aspects of what the client is communicating. The counsellor must rely on her perceptions of the client and her 'hunches' about what is going on, but at the same time be careful not to interpret what she *thinks* the client has said nor take him for granted.

Effective listening, like other skills, can be practised. When practising, be aware of the following considerations:

1. Be aware of your attitude. How do you feel about the client and how are those feelings influencing your perceptions of him?
2. Be attentive both to what is being said (content) and what is implied or hinted at (unstated or emotional message).
3. Focus on what the other person is trying to tell you, not on what you might say in response or how you can straighten out the mix-up.
4. Listening involves not only immediate understanding, but also clarifying what is obscure. Do not hesitate to say that you do not fully understand. Also, do not assume anything about your client. Ask, even if the answer seems very obvious.

Practising understanding involves 'perception-checking' which simply means that the counsellor asks the client how accurate her listening has been. The effect of perception-checking is to demonstrate interest, understanding and an openness of mind.

Exercise 4.6

Following is a list of counsellor responses or leads that can be used to see if you understood correctly. They are included to give you some ideas of how this skill can be implemented.

Is what you're saying . . .

You seem to be saying . . .

You feel . . .

As you see it . . .

Let me see if I understood correctly. You . . .; is that right?

Am I correct in assuming that you . . .

From your point of view . . .

What I hear you saying is . . .

Correct me if I'm wrong, but . . .

Using short client statements (see exercise 4.2), counsellors could use leads like those listed above to check their understanding of what has been said. In addition, the following client statements may be used for counsellors to practise accurate understanding.

(a) 'I think I can do it, but sometimes I don't know. Anyway, I guess it's worth a try.'
(b) 'I'm not sure how I feel. Sometimes I'm angry about failing; other times I just don't care. But it does bother me.'
(c) Client sits quietly, looking sad.
(d) 'I've got to get help. If you don't do something, I'll never get started.'
(e) 'Things are fine now. Thanks. I guess you won't want to see me next week.'

1. Counsellors should write their responses and then discuss them with the other members of the group to make sure that each response shows that the counsellor is trying to understand. For example, the counsellor might write the following in response to client statement (a):
   'You don't sound as though you really want to try. Is that right?'
2. When counsellors are able to write effective responses quickly and accurately, they should respond orally. Again, the responses should be discussed, so that each counsellor is sure that hers was an effective understanding check.

3. Individuals can make up client statements of their own to suit their particular work or personal situations.

EXERCISE 4.7

When listening to a dialogue or interview on television or radio, count the number of times the interviewer uses perception-checking to clarify her understanding of what the other person has said.

Leading Skills

Leading responses change the emphasis of the counselling relationship. Now the counsellor rather than the client initiates and leads. By leading, the counsellor assumes more responsibility for the discussion than the client and implies that she knows what has to be done. Leading responses should be used only when the counsellor is sufficiently sure that she understands the client's situation and needs. There is no question of the value of leading responses; instead, a counsellor must decide when they are appropriate and which one should be used.

There are certain risks associated with using leading responses. Most helpers are reasonably familiar with these skills before training. In everyday social interactions and work situations (especially teaching) leading behaviours are widely used. There may be, therefore, a tendency to over-use them or immediately to resort to them in any difficult counselling situation. Also, with reluctant or negative clients, leading responses used too soon and too frequently may irritate or seem insensitive.

INFORMATION-GIVING

There are many times when simply giving required information is the most useful thing to do. If a client asks for factual information that is directly relevant to his problem, it should be clearly, promptly and simply given.

Beginning counsellors, having learned to be wary of giving information, are sometimes reluctant to answer direct questions. They feel they should not answer until they are absolutely certain that the 'real' problem has been identified. Thus, they may be evasive and tend to probe beyond what the client has already revealed. This behaviour is irritating and confusing to the client.

Another situation that causes counsellors difficulty is when a client asks them direct, personal questions. Again, in most cases a direct, simple answer is best, even if it is a refusal to divulge the information. Clients will be more confused by and suspicious of a hesitant, evasive or equivocal reply than they will a direct refusal.

Below are examples of giving information and handling direct client questions.

1. *Client:* Has my maths teacher talked to you about me yet?
   Counsellor: No. If *you'd* like to talk to me, though, you may.
2. *Client:* What do you think I should do?
   Counsellor: Well, I don't really know. I wonder what you *want* me to say.
3. *Client:* Have you ever smoked pot?
   Counsellor: Yes, I tried it once.

In the first example, the counsellor gives a simple, negative answer to the client's question and then invites him to talk about what is on his mind. An alternative response could have been, 'No. What would the maths teacher want to talk to me about?' This is more direct and possibly more threatening to the client but potentially as effective. It is often useful to follow your direct response to the client's question with an invitation to talk or with an open question about the client's feelings or beliefs. For instance, in the second example the counsellor avoids making a decision for the client and then invites him to explore his own preferences. In the third example, the counsellor merely answers the client without any explanation and waits to see what the client's next response will be.

Giving Advice

We believe advice should be given as little as possible; only when requested, and only after careful listening has ensured that the counsellor understands the client's situation. It is a skill that is easily misused. Advice-giving is open to game-playing in that it places the counsellor in the role of expert (and all experts are sooner or later proved wrong). Also, it may be a manoeuvre by the client to avoid taking responsibility for himself or to avoid looking at an issue fully.

When advice is given, try to base it on reasons the client has previously offered in support of one particular option over others. When this is not possible, the counsellor should state the reasons why she feels a particular option is better for the client than the other options. Seeing things from this new perspective may then at least give the client feedback about himself.

Client: Even after all our talking I can't decide which to take, biology or art.
Counsellor: Well, why don't you try art. You're already taking two sciences this year, you say you want to explore other fields and you like the art teacher.

Sometimes the counsellor can use advice-giving to help a client make a decision especially if the client is still undecided after a thorough discussion of all the factors involved. Many times a person's preference becomes obvious when someone else advises another course of action.

Direct Questioning

As the name implies, direct questioning is the skill of focusing the discussion on a specific point. It is used to help clarify an issue the counsellor feels would be worth exploring further. This skill should be used sparingly until the client has been given ample opportunity to examine his situation at his own pace and in his own manner. When used, the direct question or probing question should be open rather than closed. This allows the client maximum freedom to respond and keeps the counsellor from appearing to be an interrogator.

1. *Client:* Gavin didn't keep his promise to me.
   Counsellor: (closed) Did you try reminding him of it?
   (open) How does that affect your relationship with him?
2. *Client:* Mum's OK. We get along fine. She seems to understand me. Dad's all right too, I guess.
   Counsellor: You don't seem too sure about Dad. How do you get along with him?

Influencing and Persuading

The counsellor uses these responses in an attempt to change the client's beliefs, attitudes, or behaviour. There are times when it seems that all the client needs is a 'push' to get started or make a decision. However, when used too frequently or without a complete understanding of the client's situation, attempts to persuade will usually be unsuccessful. The counsellor also risks disappointment if she too confidently believes that she knows what is best for the client, and then the client chooses another course of action. Like advice-giving, influencing is open to game-playing in that any failure can be blamed on the counsellor for offering the wrong solution.

Client: It's no use. I just don't feel comfortable in that situation.
Counsellor:
(a) I'm sure you can do it, especially if you follow the way we practised it here.
(b) If you don't, I'm afraid I can't help you any more.

Note the difference between the two counsellor responses. When would each be most effective and why?

Support and Encouragement

A less obvious form of influence is the giving of support and encouragement. Used skilfully, support and encouragement of the client as a person who is accepted and capable of coping, can be extremely reassuring and energising. Much of the feeling of support and encouragement may be conveyed non-verbally through eye contact, facial expression, smiling, posture, touch and tone of voice.

When using verbal means to convey support and encouragement, the counsellor should affirm the whole person rather than judge particular beliefs, attitudes and behaviour. If the counsellor's responses merely show approval of particular aspects of the person, there is the risk of being judgemental about what is good or bad, right or wrong for the client.

Note the differences between these three counsellor responses. Which is least judgemental and why? Which is the most obviously influencing or persuading?

Client: I have really worked at changing and I think I'm finally getting somewhere.
Counsellor:
(a) That sounds great! That's what I was hoping to hear.
(b) You sound more positive now. I'm glad to hear it.
(c) I knew you could do it; never doubted it for a minute.

Use of Personal Example or Anecdote

Sometimes it seems that it would be reassuring and supportive to a client to hear that the counsellor has experienced a similar situation and what she did to cope with it. However, we would again urge caution in using this skill. It is our experience that we have almost always regretted using personal examples. They take the focus off the client and detract from his feeling of being most important and central in the relationship. Think of a situation in which you were describing something of importance to you, and another person began telling of a similar experience of their own. How did you feel?

In the example below, however, the counsellor makes good, brief use of personal anecdote and then shifts the focus of the interview back to the client.

Client: I just can't face a group. I get nervous and forget what I am supposed to say.

Counsellor: Yes, I know that feeling well. I was so frightened of groups it almost kept me from becoming a teacher. But I'm sure that if we work on it, you can overcome your fear.

EXERCISE 4.8

The following are examples of client statements that can be used to practise each of the six leading skills discussed so far.

1. Begin by writing responses to the statements below. In groups discuss the responses so that each counsellor is sure whether hers is an effective example of the skill being practised.
2. Next, each person responds orally. Again, the group comments on the accuracy of the response as representing a specific leading skill.
3. Make up client statements of your own that are more representative of your work or personal situation.

Information-giving

(a) 'What do I have to do to enrol in this course?'
(b) 'Who do I see about applying for an emergency benefit?'
(c) 'How did I do in the group today?'

Giving Advice

(a) 'I'm finding it hard to talk with my maths teacher. What should I do?'
(b) 'I try to organise my time but somehow I never get around to actually spending time each day with the kids.'
(c) 'I just can't seem to get out of bed once I wake up. I just lie there thinking I should.'

Direct Questions

(a) 'It wasn't my fault! He's the one who should be talked to. I just gave him a bit of support.'

(b) 'Me? Oh, I'm feeling better, I guess. I just wish they would quit picking on me.'
(c) 'Nobody ever takes what I say the right way.'

Influencing or Persuading
(a) 'I don't think keeping track of how many cigarettes I smoke per day will help at all.'
(b) 'You say I should. I *know* I should. But I just can't seem to get started.'
(c) 'I don't care what happens. No teacher is going to push me around again. Next time I'll just hit him.'

Support and Encouragement
(a) 'I can't; I just can't do it. I hate having to admit it.'
(b) 'Do you really believe I can pass that exam? I hope so. I'm starting to believe it myself.'
(c) 'It's hard getting so many job refusals, but I'm not going to give up yet.'

Use of Personal Example or Anecdote
(a) 'I'll never be any good at sport.'
(b) 'I hate meeting new people. I never know what to say or how to act.'
(c) 'Sometimes I can hear myself talking but I can't stop and I end up making a fool of myself.'

INTERPRETATION

Interpretations are explanations of, or insights into, a situation. When used in counselling, they should help a client to understand the meaning of events by presenting alternative views of his problem. Interpretations will be more helpful if they arise from information the client presents rather than from the counsellor's experience and theoretical knowledge.

The counsellor should remember that an interpretation is merely one possible explanation of an event. Her client may have entirely different and equally valid explanations. The counsellor should offer interpretations tentatively, allowing the client sufficient opportunity to modify them.

Read the following counsellor interpretations. Both are based on what the client has previously said and both offer him the chance to reject or modify his statement.

1. 'From what you have said about your father, it seems that you are really very frightened of him. Is that how you see it?'

2. 'You sound as if you're extremely embarrassed about being overweight. Perhaps your aggressiveness toward others is an attempt to cover your shame. Could that be right?'

Interpretation, like many of the other leading behaviours, can have negative aspects. It can be an impersonal technique that emphasises the superior status of the counsellor. Also, too often clients will accept interpretations as factual, fatalistic explanations and cease working to change things. Offering interpretations can be valuable and necessary in counselling, but presenting them as final explanations serves only to satisfy a counsellor need, not a client need. Finally, it is our belief that a counsellor's effectiveness should never be measured by the ingeniousness or frequency of her interpretations.

Exercise 4.9

1. Think of how you felt at some point today. Try to think of as many interpretations of these feelings as you can. For example, you might begin by remembering that you felt annoyed at being misunderstood. Then try to think of all the possible explanations for that feeling (eg., 'She asked for my opinion but then didn't really seem interested – I felt foolish trying to explain.')
2. Which explanation seems to be the best? Why?

Exercise 4.10

1. Write down as many possible explanations or interpretations as you can for the first client statement below. Then discuss your interpretations with others to find out which ones satisfy the requirements of an effective interpretation (eg., based on what the client has said or directly implied, adds new meaning to the situation, presented in a way that allows the client to reject or modify it).
   (a) 'I've really messed things up with that teacher. I hate the class, the work, her. I'm really worried about my attitude.'
   (b) 'I'm finished. That factory job is too dull . . . I'm sick of putting the same piece in each crate hour after hour. I'm tired, bored, unhappy . . .'
2. Using the second client statement, respond orally with as many interpretations as you and others can think of. Discuss them to make sure they are effective interpretations.

Confrontation

Confronting is the skill of honestly and directly pointing out to the client that his description of himself or situation clearly does not match the way in which the counsellor sees the same situation. Confrontation is initiated by the counsellor. It is an expression of her own point of view rather than simply an explanation or interpretation based on one of the client's views. Confrontation can deal with such things as strengths or weaknesses a client refuses to acknowledge, misinformation or lack of information, reluctance to put a stated intention into action, or a refusal to try to see another point of view.

When confronting a client, the counsellor should focus on present feelings and behaviour and not on what the client has said or done in the past. To use this skill effectively, a counsellor must be able to:

(a) Recognise her own feelings as they occur.
(b) State those feelings clearly and simply.
(c) Tell the client her honest reaction to the behaviour or statement and the specific reasons for that reaction.
(d) Allow the client the opportunity to respond to that reaction.

Confronting involves risk, but if successful, it can greatly hasten the counselling process or overcome a block or barrier. If a helping relationship has already been developed, confrontation is less risky and may in fact be seen as challenging and helpful by the client.

For example:

1. 'You say constantly that you are going to get up on time and get to school, but you never do.'
2. 'You keep saying you love your wife, but you don't seem to want to make her happier by staying home more often.'
3. 'Right now I hear you saying things are getting better, but you have been mistaken about that twice before. What's different about this time?'

Exercise 4.11

1. Form groups of three. In each group decide who will first be counsellor, who will be client and who will be observer. The counsellor and client are to role-play the first situation given below. The counsellor is to confront the client by identifying any discrepancy that appears in what the client has been doing

or saying. The observer should make sure that the counsellor's confrontation does point out a discrepancy and does so in a way that allows the client some freedom to respond.

2. When finished, each person should swap roles and repeat the above procedure until each has had a chance to function as counsellor.

Role-play 1: You suspect the client is experiencing sexual problems in his marriage because, although the client insists there are no problems in this area, he refuses to discuss any aspect of sex and always manages to change the subject when you bring it up.

Role-play 2: The client insists he wants to change his critical and sarcastic way with people but he consistently refuses to discuss specific ways of altering this behaviour.

Role-play 3: The client keeps making negative statements about his artistic talents in spite of a number of compliments from others and praise from his art instructor.

Exercise 4.12

Think of some situation in your own life in which you could have benefitted from a challenge or confrontation. Write a statement in which you confront yourself. Choose another person with whom to share your statement. As you do this, try to be aware of how you are feeling as you do it and why. (See exercises 4.3 and 4.10)

Problem Clarification

Up to this point the whole counselling process has been aimed at establishing a trusting relationship and maintaining open communication. However, as the goal of counselling is the resolution of problems, it is important to identify exactly what the problems are and the specific means for overcoming them. To accomplish this, there are definite steps that can be followed. Below is one example of a sequence of steps to clarify a client's problem.

1. The initial aim is to identify the problem, ie., to change general problems into specific, behaviour-related problems.
   Counsellor's tasks
   (a) Clarify the meaning of general words or phrases.
   'Tell me what you mean when you say . . .'
   (b) Ask for specific examples and descriptions of circumstances.
   'Tell me of a specific instance . . .'

2. The next step is to specify alternatives, ie., what would the client prefer to happen?
   Counsellor's tasks
   (a) How would the client rather act?
       'Tell me what you would rather . . .'
   (b) What could the client do to overcome the problem?
       'How do you think you could handle . . .'

3. The client should be encouraged to explore the implications and consequences of the alternatives and to choose the most suitable.
   Counsellor's tasks
   (a) Help the client to understand advantages and disadvantages of each alternative.
       'What do you see as the advantages (disadvantages) of . . .'
   (b) Help the client make a realistic choice, ie., consider physical, emotional and social factors.
       'How are you going to choose . . .'
       'Which seems the best and why?'

4. Finally, the client should try to identify the changes or new skills that he needs to accomplish the chosen alternative.
   Counsellor's tasks
   (a) Help the client identify deficiencies.
       'What will you have to do/learn/buy etc . . .?'
   (b) Help the client take steps to overcome deficiencies.
       'Let's start by trying . . .'

EXERCISE 4.13

1. The group divide into pairs and decide who will play the role of counsellor and who will play the client. Using one of the role-play situations described below, the counsellor leads the client through the four-step problem clarification sequence described above. The counsellor should move from one stage to the next only when the first step has been satisfactorily covered.
2. When finished, the participants should swap roles and repeat the role-play situation below.
3. When both persons have played counsellor, discuss the usefulness of the problem clarification sequence in the larger group setting. For example, people

may want to comment on how easy the sequence was to follow, how useful it was as a guide or indicator of progress, or its relevance to a real counselling situation.

Role-play 1: The client begins by saying he would like to be more at ease in groups.
Role-play 2: The client says that his children are able to manipulate him too easily.

SUMMARISING

Summarising is the process of tying together all that has been communicated during part or all of the counselling session. It attempts to bring together the main highlights of what has occurred thereby clarifying what has been accomplished and what remains to be done. Summarising also serves as a natural means of finishing a session or beginning a new one.

It is often effective to have the client summarise what has happened or been discussed. This enables the counsellor to get a better understanding of the client's view of things and helps the client see what progress has been made.

When summarising, the counsellor should try to pull together the most salient points, state them as simply and clearly as possible and ask the client for his reaction to the accuracy of the summary.

For example:

Counsellor: Let's see if we can put all of this together. On the one hand you feel lonely and isolated, especially with groups of people. On the other hand, you say that you find it hard to mix with others even on a one-to-one basis. So, even though you want to get to know others, there is no easy way to begin. Is that it?

EXERCISE 4.14

Discuss a topic with a partner. The topic should be something of concern or interest to both people. Note that this need not be a role-play situation in which one person is designated counsellor and the other client.

Every few minutes ask someone (the leader, trainer, or a person designated as time-keeper) to interrupt and ask that each person attempt to summarise what has happened to that point. Before allowing discussion to continue, make sure that each person agrees that his partner's summary is accurate.

Exercise 4.15

Notice how often the interviewer in a radio or television news or current affairs panel discussion uses the skill of summarising.

Review Exercise 4.16

In order to review the skills in chapters 3 and 4, make two or three lists of five different skills each. Then role-play an interview with another person and try to use each of the skills from one list in a five minute interview. Ask an observer to check that each skill has been used. Repeat using the other lists of skills.

Summary

By using various responding and leading skills, the counsellor in the middle stages of counselling helps the client to become as clear as possible about his problems or concerns. This paves the way for the client to commit himself to taking action to reduce or solve these problems.

5

Changing Behaviour Through Counselling

If the skills described in the two previous chapters have been put into practice, the counsellor will have helped clients considerably. Problems will have been clarified objectively, emotional reactions will have been explored, and various alternatives and their consequences will have been considered. For some clients such help may be enough; they may feel ready to make plans and to take new steps without further help.

Clients often need more direct assistance, however, if they are to follow through from gaining greater insight and self-understanding to reaching practical solutions. Effective counselling usually means helping someone to be different in some distinctive way. It means helping someone to behave differently – to do different things, to talk in new ways, perhaps to stop some well established habit, or to feel and think differently about themselves.

General Principles

Certain general principles are useful in helping clients to change. Sometimes they are sufficient in themselves, but sometimes they need to be supplemented by specific techniques such as those described later in this chapter.

Giving Directions or Suggestions

An obvious, but essential skill in helping clients to act or to change is the ability to give simple, clear directions or suggestions, using language the client understands. Giving clients precise directions can occur at any stage of the counselling process but is most often used when helping someone to practise a new behaviour or initiate change. For example, while some clients might readily respond to 'Close your eyes and go with the energy flow', others may respond more readily to 'Close your eyes, sit in a position that feels relaxed, and just let your thoughts come and go. Do not try to control them'. In order to be effective, directions and suggestions must be brief, understandable and perceived by the client to be relevant to the subject of discussion.

Exercise 5.1

As counsellor, give clear, simple directions so that the client can:
(a) Play the role of her angry mother.
(b) Adopt a more assertive posture.

Setting Goals

Some clients express their goals in vague general terms. In the behaviour-change phase of counselling the first job of the counsellor is to get his client to be clear and specific about her goals. He may do this by helping her to break a general goal into smaller more manageable ones, to plan practical steps towards a goal, or to choose one main goal from a number of desired ones.

A useful technique to assist goal-setting is to encourage the client to think of alternative ways of behaving. This forces her to be practical. For example, the counsellor could ask, 'What do you want to do differently?' or, 'You're getting upset at the way your children react to you. What would you like them to do instead?' Answers may come in the form of goals such as these: 'Have more fun with the children.' 'Be able to study better.' 'Avoid nagging.'

Helpful though these goals are, each should be made still more precise. 'More fun with the children' might come to be defined in several different ways – having a game with them for at least 20 minutes every day, or swapping a joke every morning, or reading a story every evening. One of these should then be chosen as the first goal. The goal of 'more effective study' might be specified as reading and taking notes without a break for 40 minutes at least twice a day. Negative goals such as 'stop nagging' need to be put in positive terms, so that there is something definite to aim for. 'Stop nagging' might then be changed into making a request pleasantly, very specifically, with careful timing, and once only.

Exercise 5.2*

1. Label each of the following as either 'G' (a general goal) or 'S' (a specific behaviour): (a) playing poker; (b) being a good conversationalist; (c) feeling on top of the world; (d) asking open-ended questions; (e) improving work habits; (f) relaxing in the evenings; (g) inviting two friends to lunch; (h) driving the car; (i) feeling competent; (j) standing no nonsense; (k) doing yoga for 5 minutes daily; (l) setting the table. Check the answers at the end of the book and discuss them with others.
2. Write down one particular behaviour that might lead to each of these goals: (a) losing weight; (b) improving my appearance; (c) standing up to my mother; (d) getting fit; (e) not boring other people; (f) controlling the class better; (g) getting on top of the job; (h) taking a break. For each goal list the behaviours suggested by the group.

Gaining Commitment

The client's motivation to change her behaviour is a major factor in counselling. It is best if she chooses and specifies her own goal, for she is then more likely to work hard to achieve it. But a counsellor who has developed a good working relationship with a client should not hesitate to offer suggestions as a way of prompting her thinking. He should ensure, however, that she commits herself fully to her goal and that she accepts responsibility for it. If the counsellor neglects to do this, the client may blame him for any failure. The counsellor should take care that the client commits herself to a goal that she sees as being realistic and desirable, and one into which she is prepared to put time and effort.

In getting such a commitment from the client, several of the leading and responding skills will be important. The skill of influencing might be needed to convince those who give up easily and who express fatalistic attitudes, saying, 'It's just hereditary – my mother was exactly the same.' Without pushing too hard, the counsellor should give one or two carefully chosen examples, using ordinary language and citing details that seem close to her situation: 'Many parents have been able to stop children's temper tantrums in just a week or so, and without getting upset themselves.'

Sometimes a client's reactions to a counsellor's attempt to get her to specify goals might contradict her stated aims. In such a case confrontation might be an appropriate technique: 'You tell me that you want to be able to talk to your boyfriend on more equal terms, but you still haven't come up with any topic that you're willing to start on, and you've objected to every suggestion I've made.' Obviously, the success of such a response by the counsellor will depend upon his having established an open and honest relationship with his client earlier.

The counsellor might find it helpful to formalise an agreement beyond the client's oral statement. If a client finds it very difficult to bring herself to act in a certain situation, asking her to write down her plan in simple direct language could be useful. She could even be asked to sign and date a written statement or contract, for example: 'I agree to practise how I will enter the room, sit down, move about, present myself, and talk to the group. I will do this three times this week just before each meeting. After each meeting I will write down all the things I did well and also those things I still need to work on. I will bring this record to the next session and talk about it.'

Notice that this contract sets out:

1. Exactly what the client is to do.
2. How often she will do it.
3. How it will be used at the next session.

Such contracts should be planned jointly by the counsellor and his client. Provided that the task is relevant to her problem and is realistic and simple, then carrying it out will be satisfying to her. It is important that the client is motivated and actively participates in changing her behaviour. Requiring her to plan and execute tasks in this way ensures her involvement.

Exercise 5.3

1. Role-play in counsellor/client pairs. The client's role is to express doubts about being able to do certain things. Assume that the client has little formal education. Give the exact words you would use to convince her that it is possible to learn to:
   (a) Stop children's temper tantrums.
   (b) Ask for help from a welfare agency.
   (c) Refuse overtime work.
   (d) Make a complaint to a teacher.
   (e) Ask that something borrowed be returned.
   (f) Return unsatisfactory goods to a shop.

(g) Ask for a small favour.
(h) Cut short a boring conversation.

2. In pairs plan a contract which follows the three basic rules. Choose any topics, eg., a physical fitness programme, a new way of doing a routine chore.

Anticipating Situations

Having gained his client's commitment to a precise goal, the counsellor's next job is to help her to plan exactly how, when, and where the change process will start in earnest. She should be made aware of the many factors that contribute to success. Among these is the importance of first practising only in those situations in which the chances of success are very good.

Everything should be planned carefully. She should be helped to choose the best time and place to start, to decide exactly what to say and do, to imagine how she wants to look and feel, to consider likely reactions of others, and of herself, and to anticipate her response to these different reactions. Such matters should be fully discussed so that the client feels very secure in what she is planning to do. The counsellor should encourage her to anticipate success, even if it might be unpleasant for her to think about the situation beforehand.

The prospect of failure should also be discussed, because it would be foolish of the counsellor to guarantee success. While the emphasis should be on the positive aspects and on planning for success, the client should be encouraged to think of failure as 'nothing lost', and as an opportunity to make better plans for the next occasion.

Exercise 5.4

Write out a detailed plan to handle each of the following tasks. In each case try to anticipate what could possibly happen and work out a plan to deal with each (eg., If he says this, I'll say that):

1. Declining an invitation that you expect to be given face-to-face and in a very pressing manner.
2. Expressing first your doubts about, then your firm opposition to, something you had previously agreed to.
3. Talking in an interview with a domineering supervisor about two aspects of your job that you want to see altered.

Discuss each plan with a partner.

Assessing Results

As soon as possible after the client has carried out a behaviour change plan, the counsellor should discuss the experience with her. The factors that contributed to success should be identified so that she will be encouraged to try again. The sequence of events leading up to the episode and the details of the episode itself should be recounted. The counsellor should also discuss with the client how she felt, and remind her of the satisfactions she achieved. She should be encouraged to re-experience those pleasant feelings as vividly as possible, as these will act as inducements for her to repeat her first success.

The value of repetition and practice should be stressed and the client should be urged to repeat the task as often as necessary. If she is hesitant, the counsellor should remind her of the 'pay-offs' she is getting for her performance.

Exercise 5.5

In pairs, one person tells of an actual or imagined experience in which the outcome was successful, but about which there had been considerable uncertainty and anxiety beforehand. Begin with an example from the previous exercise. The other person asks questions that bring out reasons for the success. Then reverse the roles.

Making Records

Recording is a simple but very important skill because it provides one of the most powerful means of prompting behaviour change. The client who feels that she accomplishes little should be urged to keep a detailed diary of how she spends her day. The parent who complains about her child's misbehaviour or the teacher concerned about an unruly class should each be helped to organise a recording system showing what happens just before and just after each misbehaviour and also how often the misbehaviours occur.

Recording should be focused on one or two observable behaviours that are at the centre of the issue and that can be counted. Observations based on generalised behaviours and vague problems lead to useless records. It is impossible to get accurate information about things like inattentiveness, over-eating, disobedience, or poor communication without being precise about what these descriptions mean and how they are exemplified. Counsellors should help clients to clarify the problem by asking them specific questions: 'What exactly was consumed between each meal in each 24-hour period?' 'How many questions did you ask in that time?' 'How many times was she out of her seat during the lesson?'

Recording is hardly a counselling skill, but it is such a valuable aid to making good decisions about change that its importance must be stressed. Counsellors should urge clients to gather relevant information about their behaviour and the behaviour of others when considering behaviour change. In some instances keeping an impersonal, accurate record can induce change without the use of any other skills or methods.

EXERCISE 5.6

1. Choose a familiar TV advertisement and practise recording one behaviour, eg., How often is the name of the product or service presented? List all the adjectives used. How often does the model's head move? How many different camera shots are used?
2. Watch two people talking together. In different one-minute segments, record separate behaviours, one to each segment, eg., number of head movements, leg movements, arm movements. Compare your record with that of a partner.
3. Imagine that you are finding it difficult to fit everything into your day. Make a log of your activities yesterday from getting up to going to bed. Describe the activities in detail. Keep the log in at least half-hour segments. Explain to a partner in what respects this was a typical day, and in what respects it was unusual.

Specific Techniques

It is often necessary for the counsellor to help a client to try out different ways of behaving. He can do this by the way he talks to her and also by teaching her new behaviours which she can practise during counselling and in her ordinary activities.

USING REWARDS

There is much current interest in finding out how to change people's behaviour in various settings (families, work places, schools, institutions) by systematically altering the associations between events or 'bits' of behaviour. The general name for this method of changing behaviour is *reinforcement,* which refers to the way in which one can increase or decrease the likelihood that certain events will occur. As a general rule, behaviour which is regularly and immediately followed by pleasant experiences tends to be repeated. Such behaviour is said to be rewarded or positively reinforced. On the other hand, behaviour which is ignored or has unpleasant consequences becomes less likely to reappear.

In everyday life things often seem to be more complicated than that and to follow either different rules or no rules at all. This is partly because what is rewarding to one person in a particular setting may not be so to others in that setting or to the same person in a different setting. Generally, however, the apparent complexities and contradictions arise from the fact that we have not observed accurately enough what is in fact occurring. For example, the very threats and naggings that are intended to stop a child's misbehaviour at home or at school, frequently have the opposite effect. In an apparently perverse way they serve to reinforce the unwanted behaviour. This is because misbehaviour is all that the adult has responded to, and the child gets little or no recognition or reward for good behaviour. Frequently in such a situation all desirable behaviour passes unnoticed and without commendation of any kind, and the only adult reaction (notice, even in the form of nagging) is to misbehaviour. The most effective way of dealing with a child who is misbehaving is by ignoring this if possible, and instead making pleasant comments about appropriate behaviour. This must be done immediately after it occurs, so that the desired behaviour is reinforced. Parents and teachers using such tactics for the first time are often startled at their effectiveness.

Counsellors should help clients to plan changes based on careful observation of exactly 'what is reinforcing what'. The combination of rewarding desired behaviour and ignoring inappropriate behaviour is especially powerful, although it may not be sufficient or appropriate in every case. It is nevertheless widely applicable; problems arising in groups, in family relationships, and in supervision or training situations can often be resolved by altering the reinforcements in this manner. (Krumboltz and Thoresen describe how to treat more difficult problems. See the Select Bibliography.)

Most of the counselling techniques used in the beginning and developing stages include rewarding effects. Good eye-contact and other minimal encouragers are rewarding in that they help a client to feel accepted and induce her to keep talking. Topic-following and reflection of feeling have similar effects. Almost all techniques in the early stages reward intimacy, sharing, problem-exploration, and a search for solutions.

But there is another aspect of reward which the counsellor can use to get his client to focus on some matters rather than on others. A good counsellor uses his techniques selectively in a manner similar to that of the successful teacher or parent, reinforcing certain remarks and ignoring others. In this way he can effectively influence the course of a counselling session, for those client remarks to which he refers in any way (except a strongly disapproving one) tend to be enlarged upon, while those he ignores tend to be dropped. By talking about or showing interest in client remarks which refer to insights and plans for instance, the counsellor is rewarding problem-solving and positive attitudes. If at the same time the counsellor ignores or cuts off long complaints and harrowing tales (ie., does not reward them), he is discouraging irresponsibility, and is in effect saying, 'I don't want to hear any more war stories. Let's see what we can actually do about this problem.' (It is possible for the counsellor to ignore something that the client particularly wants to talk about. In a good relationship the effects of such a misjudgement can usually be overcome, for the client will raise the topic again if it is important to her.)

Simple counselling techniques with strong reward components are appropriate skills to teach to some clients. For example, a client lacking in conversational ability might be coached by the counsellor in basic attending skills. Used in social situations, these skills act as rewards to speakers who are thus encouraged to respond to the client by conversing with her. A client should be urged to practise such skills in her own time and to report on their effects. Responding skills would likewise be valuable as general social skills.

The counsellor should remember that reward techniques can operate in either direction, and that a client may use them on the counsellor, as well as vice versa.

Another useful reward technique involves getting the client to make a list of satisfying activities for herself, or for another person for whom she feels responsible. At first her list might include only the following: tending plants, chatting on the phone, walking the dog, listening to a record. Her adolescent son or daughter might have a list like this: having a driving lesson, playing pool, going to a disco. In both instances at least a dozen items should be listed. The list can be regarded as a kind of menu from which many satisfying activities can be selected.

All these activities can then be used either as rewards to be enjoyed *after* a certain disliked task has been performed, or as substitutes – *instead of* some self-defeating behaviour. In the first instance the satisfaction of a coffee break or a driving lesson might be made to depend upon having done all chores or studied for two 40-minute periods. In the latter case a client may be urged to consult the list and choose an activity whenever she feels that she is becoming tense, or bored, or depressed. Thus, instead of sinking further into unpleasant thoughts and feelings, she might invite a friend to lunch or go out to the shop, and thus counter her depression or boredom.

Exercise 5.7

1. *Selective reinforcement*

   Notice that each of the following client statements includes references to both feeling and an action that might be taken. Identify both parts of each statement, and then make up a simple reflection comment that reinforces the action part. For example:

Client: I get so annoyed! They just won't do what I tell them!
Counsellor: You would like them to co-operate with you more?

   (a) 'Actually I am pretty low just now. I wish I could get more work done.'
   (b) 'I can't seem to talk to my old man these days. He really makes me mad.'
   (c) 'My husband and I just don't do things together any more Perhaps we're bored with each other.'

2. *Reinforcement menus*

   Make a list of activities that might be satisfying to you if you were in each of these situations:

   (a) A young mother with two children under three years, living in a new suburb.
   (b) A 16-year-old apprentice mechanic, boarding away from home.
   (c) A woman recently widowed, no family, 45 years old.
   (d) A retired farmer living in a big city.

   For each situation make a composite list from everyone's contributions.

Providing Models

Modelling means providing a good example or pattern of behaviour for the client who does not know how to act appropriately in some situation. At one level, of course, modelling could mean simply showing a physical example, eg., a client's note-taking might be improved by seeing a sample page done by a fellow student.

Counsellors should be alert to opportunities for helping clients in such simple ways.

Usually, however, modelling refers to actions which seem very complicated but which do not result in a product like a page of notes. For this reason modelling is commonly demonstrated in two ways – both completely, without a break, to show the total effect, and also in segments so that the separate skills can be isolated for observation and practice. The counsellor can act as a model in his office. A peer or colleague of the client can act as a model for her in the client's ordinary social setting. A model can also take the form of a special presentation of the behaviour, eg., film or videotape.

There are some obvious advantages and disadvantages to these alternatives. The most serious disadvantage is that the performance of the peer or colleague cannot be controlled or repeated. It is best if the counsellor can emphasise the vital parts of the performance and repeat those that he wishes to underline still further. Slight exaggeration can sometimes help in emphasising salient points.

After the model has been presented, the client should be asked to attempt to imitate the model. She should then be encouraged to rehearse the behaviour, with the counsellor giving her immediate feedback in the form of positive comments and suggestions about needed improvements. She should be reminded of the importance of such *behaviour rehearsal* in her own time.

The procedure for effective modelling may be summarised thus:

1. Ask the client to demonstrate how she typically acts.
2. Isolate effective and ineffective parts of her behaviour for observation, discussion and practise.
3. Choose one or two of the ineffective behaviours and demonstrate a more effective way.
4. Repeat the demonstration several times if necessary, exaggerating the parts that cause difficulty.
5. Ask the client to rehearse the behaviour she has observed. Give her helpful feedback.
6. Continue rehearsing until a smooth, natural performance is achieved.
7. Repeat this process with other, more complex aspects of the client's behaviour.

When using modelling, it is important to begin with simple aspects of the client's behaviour. This helps to ensure that the client will experience success and improvement and will thus be willing and confident to attempt more complex behaviours. It is usually easier for clients to master simple non-verbal skills before attempting more complex verbal skills.

Part of a good modelling session might go something like this: 'Remember each point. You must always knock firmly. When he calls "Come in", stand up straight, push the door open, step into the room, look straight at him and smile. Got that? . . . Now before we go any further, you repeat those points to me . . . Good, now we'll both say them again, out loud, while you watch me do it. See, first I . . . then I . . . OK? Now, you try it while we both repeat the steps aloud once more . . . Very good. You did this, this, this, and this perfectly. But next time, up straighter and a bit firmer on the door knocking.'

Exercise 5.8

Plan modelling sessions with your partner, breaking up each of the following situations into two or three segments, each containing specific behaviours. Consider every detail – appearance, timing, gestures, posture, sequences, words, tone, facial expression. Then carry out each modelling segment, with your partner giving feedback on your performance.

(a) Entering an office to ask for a job.
(b) Facing a reputedly tough class for the first time.
(c) Making a complaint about a purchase.
(d) Rebuking someone who has jumped a queue.

Role-Playing

Role-playing means acting out how a person with a particular title or function usually behaves. It is obviously akin to modelling and behaviour rehearsal, and all three are often used in conjunction with one another. But role-playing usually implies a less prescribed way of behaving. The emphasis is more upon feeling what it is like to act in a certain manner, sometimes with the further implication that the role, being different, is unfamiliar. The roles should not be played for long; three or four minutes is all that is necessary.

Some examples might help. A teacher plays a different role from a student, as does a nurse from a patient, and a counsellor or social worker from a client. If people pair off, play one of these roles and then switch to the other, ie., *reverse roles,* they might begin to experience what another person feels or thinks. As a result, those taking part would probably be better able to appreciate what actually goes on in such pairings. If they are professionals, such learning may help them to be more effective in their work.

The many opportunities for direct learning in role-playing and role reversal make them practical skills for counsellors to use in helping clients to change. These skills would be appropriate for a counsellor wishing to assist an adolescent girl who wanted to talk to her mother in a more adult fashion. He might first encourage her to try out several different ways of doing this while he played a parental role according to her instructions. She would thus be helped to experiment with alternatives within a safe setting. If both counsellor and client were then to reverse roles, the girl might thus, by acting out feelings and hunches, be able to anticipate more accurately how her mother might respond to the different approaches.

In both role-playing and role reversal the client should be encouraged, even coached, to throw herself into the parts she plays, with all the feelings, gestures, words, tones, and volume that are typically used, or that she wants to experiment with. The more convincingly the roles are enacted, the greater the number of learning opportunities and change possibilities that are offered to the client.

Exercise 5.9

Try short role-plays and role reversals for each of these situations:
(a) mother – daugher conflict
(b) worker – supervisor interview
(c) housewife – door-to-door salesman
(d) teacher – student conference about unsatisfactory work
(e) nurse – patient exchange about medicine not taken
(f) welfare agency receptionist – applicant for assistance
(g) minister – recently deserted wife

Bodily Awareness, Relaxation, Activities

As part of the processes by which behaviour is changed, it can be very helpful for people to become more aware of and in control of their bodily sensations. Heightened awareness can help clients to identify their feelings more precisely. Take, for example, a client who says she feels childish when spoken to patronisingly.

'What do you mean, patronisingly?'

'Well, he says things like – "Typical woman, over-reacting again!"

'So you feel childish. How do you react physically, then?'

'I get all churned up inside. I feel my face getting red, and I want to scream at him.'

Counsellors can make much use of such material, getting clients to 'tune into' and then act out bodily feelings as a way of reporting their typical behaviour.

Bodily awareness techniques can also be used to help clients to gain more control of themselves. Relaxation is an especially useful skill for this. Transcendental meditation, yoga, biofeedback, and hypnosis are other examples of techniques with similar purposes. The advantages of relaxation are that it is easily taught and easily learned. In addition, relaxation can conveniently be used in a wide variety of real-life situations. It can also be useful as an adjunct to other counselling skills.

Relaxation is achieved by gradually loosening muscles in all parts of the body so that there is no tightness or tension anywhere. Full attention is required, so that different parts of the body are relaxed in sequence. It is possible to attain either complete relaxation, so that the whole body is limp, or partial relaxation, which can be used as a way of coping with particular tensions, for example in the neck or stomach. Different degrees or levels of relaxation can be reached, from simply removing muscle tension to attaining a state of rest approximating sleep, sometimes in fact going to sleep.

A counsellor who senses that his client is very anxious while talking to him may help her to relax by getting her to do a few simple exercises. This may help her to face her problems more calmly in counselling.

'How about just leaning right back in the chair and taking three or four deep breaths . . . Slowly now, fill up your lungs . . . Slower yet, just relax your arms . . .'

She may be encouraged to relax in these ways in her ordinary life.

Relaxation can be used in preparing for some especially tense situation, such as an interview, examination, or important meeting. Counsellors should encourage clients to use partial relaxation skills while actually in tense situations. It can also be a satisfying respite after a worrying or upsetting experience or physical exertion.

The following set of directions is typical of those used to attain a deep state of relaxation. Counsellors who often use relaxation methods usually have such directions readily available for clients in pamphlet form and recorded on cassette tapes, with the instructions paced slowly enough to last about 20 minutes.

1. Lie flat on the back, placing the feet about 18 inches apart. The hands should rest lightly away from the trunk, with the palms up.
2. Close your eyes and gently move all the different parts of the body to create a general feeling of relaxation.
3. Then start relaxing the body part by part. First think of the right leg. Inhale and slowly raise the leg about one foot off the floor. Hold it fully tensed. After five seconds, exhale abruptly and relax the muscles of the right leg, allowing it to fall to the floor on its own. Shake the leg gently from right to left, relax it fully, and forget about the existence of this leg.
4. Repeat this same process with the left leg, and then with both hands, one at a time.
5. Then bring the mind to the muscles of the pelvis, buttocks, and anus. Tense them and relax. Once again, tense them and relax. Next, think of the abdomen. Inhale deeply through the nose and bloat the abdomen. Hold your breath for five seconds and suddenly let the air burst out through the mouth, simultaneously relaxing all the muscles of the abdomen and diaphragm.
6. Move up to the chest region. Inhale deeply through the nose, bloating the chest. Hold your breath for five seconds and suddenly let the air out through the mouth while relaxing all the muscles of the chest and diaphragm.
7. Move on to the shoulders. Without moving the forearms off the floor, try to make the shoulders meet in front of the body. Then relax and let them drop to the floor.
8. Slowly, gently, turn the neck right and left, right and left, then back to centre, mentally relaxing the neck muscles.
9. Coming to the facial muscles, move the jaw up and down, left and right a few times, then relax. Squeeze the lips together in a pout, then relax. Suck in the cheek muscles, then relax. Tense the tip of the nose, then relax. Wrinkle the forehead muscles, then relax.
10. Now you have relaxed all the muscles of the body. To make sure of this, allow your mind to wander over your entire body from the tips of the toes to the

> head, searching for any spots of tension. If you come across any spots of tension, concentrate upon this part and it will relax. If you do this mentally, without moving any muscle, you will notice that the part concerned obeys your command.

This is complete relaxation. Even your mind is at rest now. You may keep watching your breath, which will keep flowing in and out quite freely and calmly. Observe your thoughts without trying to take your mind anywhere. You are a witness, not a body or a mind but an ocean of peace and tranquillity. Remain in this condition at least five minutes. Do not become anxious about anything. When you decide to wake from this conscious sleep, do so quite slowly. Imagine that fresh energy is gently entering each part of your body, from the head down to the toes. Then slowly sit up. This exercise helps create a refreshed and peaceful feeling for the body and mind. Try to do this one to three times a day, especially upon rising and before retiring.*

The reduction of tension by taking up some physical activity should also be recognised as a useful way of helping clients to change their behaviour. A game that demands some exertion of energy and permits some social interaction reduces tension and can serve as an excellent reward. However, solitary active pursuits may be preferred by some. Physical activities can reduce the many stresses that come from modern living – mentally and emotionally demanding experiences and boring, solitary, and sedentary occupations. Similar functions can be served by many other pursuits such as dancing, hobbies, games, arts and crafts, and playing and listening to music. It would be wise to encourage clients to include in every 'reinforcement menu' some physical or creative activity.

Exercise 5.10

In pairs or in a small group practise the 10 steps to relaxation described above. Discuss the experience, and list possible uses you may find for relaxation.

Thoughts and Imagery

A counsellor's ability to deal directly and constructively with his client's mental activity is another important counselling skill. The client's thoughts, ideas, and

* These directions for relaxation are reprinted by special permission of the Rodale Press Inc., Emmaus, Pennyslvania.

perceptions are obviously important throughout counselling, so much so that their uses in changing behaviour are often overlooked. A good example of how imagery can be used is shown by the ways in which relaxation is taught. Besides the usual method of directing his client to relax various muscle groups, the counsellor may encourage her to recall or imagine events and situations which help the physical processes. This imagery encourages the loosening of her muscle tension. Physical tightness in her body may be reduced if she can call up images associated with calm, comfort, and rest. The counsellor prompts her to do this by using colourful language and a suitable tone of voice:

'Imagine you are on soft cushions in a dimly lit room with quiet slow music.'

'Notice how slow, and deep, and easy your breathing is now.'

'Feel all the tightness easing away as though you were in a warm bath.'

At various points in a counselling relationship, thinking and imagination can be profitably used to help the change process. For example, the counsellor should encourage his client to use similar sorts of descriptions and language to fill out what she means by such general terms as 'a real scene', 'not so good', 'feeling better'. He should try to get her to think, imagine, and describe things in concrete and colourful detail in response to such questions and requests as these:

1. 'Tell me how you're feeling right now, when you're saying that you feel trapped. What does your body seem to be saying to you?'
2. 'What does he do then? How do you think he feels at those moments? And how do you feel when he says and does those things?'

Some clients seem to have too active an imagination, and most of their difficulties seem to arise from the way they concentrate on negative aspects of their thoughts. These people become more and more anxious and resistant to change because they constantly anticipate failure, and as a result they avoid facing up to things. In whatever ways he can, the counsellor should stop the clients from dwelling on these aspects. He can reinforce talk about alternatives, he can ignore references to negative aspects, and he can point out in a rational manner the self-defeating nature of such thoughts. He can also elicit from his client 'reinforcement menus' of images which have pleasant associations, and to which she can be urged to turn whenever negative images intrude. Such a programme of 'guided fantasy' would of course need to be supported and supplanted as soon as possible by more active steps to bring the images into reality.

A rather dramatic technique called *thought-stopping* is a further example of the use that some counsellors make of the clients' mental activities in trying to change their behaviour. It is sometimes used to help clients who constantly engage in unproductive talk. If, for example, the client begins expressing her doubts or fears for the tenth time, the counsellor might interrupt her. He might say firmly, 'Stop that, right now!' and emphasise his point with a gross movement such as thumping his chair, or standing up, or turning away. By this means he might succeed in directing her to talk about something else that could lead to constructive action.

Obviously the success of such a technique depends upon a sound counsellor-client relationship and upon good judgement by the counsellor. An extension of this technique is sometimes useful. If the counsellor should find that certain situations seem to prompt negative thoughts in the client, he might encourage her to devise a thought-stopping signal for herself. It might be in the form of a note in a conspicuous place that says, 'Stop complaining!' or 'Don't apologise!'

Exercise 5.11

As counsellor, plan how you would encourage a client (your partner) to think positively, and in concrete detail about:

(a) Cooking a special evening meal for the family.
(b) Going to bed in a relaxed way.
(c) Getting ready for work on a Monday.
(d) Having a relative to stay for a week when it does not really suit.

Desensitisation

This approach to changing behaviour uses several techniques together, including thinking, relaxing, and imagining. In effect the counsellor tries to inoculate the client against fears and anxieties that have become very intense in a particular situation. He does this by using the client's relaxed bodily state to counter the tensed bodily sensations that arise when she recalls situations in which she was frightened or anxious. There are several considerations and distinct stages in the process.

1. The technique is most appropriately used with clients who are anxious about only one specific matter, eg., examination fears, a dread about aircraft, or fear of blood.

2. Before beginning, the process should be fully explained to the client and her feelings about it explored. Unless she accepts that change is possible and that most fears are learned and can be unlearned, the process will not work.
3. First the client must learn to relax deeply when instructed or at will.
4. The next step is for the counsellor and client together to work out a list of the events that are associated with the fear. These are then sorted into a series (or hierarchy) from least feared to most feared. The least feared are usually those most remote in time and place from the situation of major concern.

   A hierarchy of examination fear might begin with 'thinking about the exam three weeks beforehand', and end with 'sitting in the exam room picking up the paper'. Since the hierarchy is important, the counsellor should try to elicit at least 10 items from the client. It can be useful to try sorting them on to a scale, assigning a value of 0 to the least and 100 to the very worst, and filling in as many of the intermediate values as possible. The thinking and imagining involved in this stage are very important parts of the process.
5. In the next stage the counsellor first helps the client to achieve a state of deep physical relaxation by adding as much mentally relaxing imagery as possible. Then he describes the lowest item in the fear hierarchy to her. If she signals that it is distressing to imagine that item (eg., by raising a finger), he helps her to relax and concentrate on other pleasant images until she feels able to cope. Not giving a signal means that she can tolerate that item. He then introduces the next item.
6. In this way the two of them gradually work up the hierarchy. The counsellor urges the client to practise the essentials of the technique in her own time, and to do whatever she can to support herself in the real situation when the anxiety occurs (eg., deep breathing, partial relaxation, thought-stopping).

Exercise 5.12

In counsellor-client pairs, the client talks about (a) a pleasant, exciting experience, and (b) an extremely unpleasant experience. As counsellor, help the client to describe the details of each experience as vividly as possible. Try to arrange the details of each experience into a hierarchy from least pleasant (unpleasant) to most pleasant. Try to spread the items on a scale from 0 to 100.

Mixing Strategies

Desensitisation is a notable example of a technique which involves several different counselling skills in combination. Once the various separate skills of counselling and change processes have been mastered, counsellors are urged to combine them as they see fit. Many combinations are possible, and books on counselling often describe these as mixed or multiple strategies.

Skills developed by gestalt counsellors exemplify such approaches well by combining imagery, bodily awareness, and role-playing. Assertion training schemes likewise show how counsellors can help people by using a mixture of strategies. Typically such training involves the use of rational planning, imagery, modelling and role-playing, followed by careful rehearsal of actions, words, and feelings. The result is that people who usually are not able to say what they want to because of being either too timid or too domineering, learn to express themselves more effectively.

Review Exercise 5.13

1. Using a verbatim transcript of a counselling interview, identify the skills used in every counsellor lead. Compare your answers with those of others. This exercise will help you to review many of the skills discussed in the previous three chapters and will indicate those about which there is still some uncertainty.
2. With the client's permission, record a counselling interview using an audio recorder. Analyse the interview as follows:
   (a) Transcribe verbatim two sets of 15 consecutive interactions from any two sections of the interview.
   (b) Critically analyse the transcribed portions of the interview by identifying the skill used, its intended effect and its actual effect. In addition, look for patterns of skill usage, indications of a typical style, and any inappropriate leads or assumptions that influence the course of the interview.

   This exercise can be repreated over time. It can serve as a check on one's progress, proficiency and effectiveness. See the example on page 128.
3. Make a brief video or audio programme illustrating the effective use of a skill or skills. This is an excellent way of demonstrating a working understanding of particular counselling skills.

Ending Contact

The counsellor should recognise that ending a counselling relationship through referral or termination entails certain procedures and obligations.

Referral

If the counsellor decides that his client has needs that he cannot meet, he should consider referring her to another agency or individual. Assuming that he has first appraised his client's needs carefully, he should adopt the following principles and procedures.

1. The counsellor should first find out whether another agency provides the necessary services. This requires a thorough knowledge of community resources for helping (eg., employment, residential care, medical, recreational, rehabilitative, educational), including their policies, programmes, costs, and limitations. It is also important to know agencies' rules and all relevant statutory obligations.
2. Having selected an appropriate agency, the counsellor should then discuss the case with the person in the agency who would probably receive the referral, taking care, however, not to disclose confidential information about his client.
3. If a referral seems appropriate, it should then be discussed with the client. The counsellor should prepare her for it, explaining honestly and clearly his decision to refer her to that particular agency. He should encourage her to react to the proposal and, if possible, to participate in the actual decision. He should also take into account the possibility that she may think that her problem is insoluble if he cannot help her further.
4. When a referral has been agreed upon, definite arrangements should be made so that the client knows exactly when and where to go and whom to ask for. In some cases the counsellor might decide to accompany the client on the first occasion.
5. The counsellor should take care to provide the agency with relevant information about the client, including:
   (a) a clear statement of her problem or needs;
   (b) a summary of the help that has been given;
   (c) a request for a specific service for her;
   (d) an indication of her feelings about referral.

6. After the referral has been completed, the counsellor should be prepared to co-operate in some way if asked to do so by the referral agency. Whether he continues to be actively involved in the case or not, he should seek a progress report from the agency so that he can assess the usefulness of the referral.

In all decisions regarding referral, the counsellor should be guided by his estimate of his client's best interests. In dealing with her, he should continue to be open, honest, and supportive, and he should act only with her consent.

Termination

Termination may occur at any time – most obviously when the objectives of the counselling relationship have been reached. It may also result from an agreement at the outset that only one topic or problem would be dealt with, or that there would be a specified number of sessions.

Besides estimating the client's readiness to cope alone, the counsellor should be aware of his own reactions. It is understandable that a counsellor would regret losing contact with a client who, for instance, had been pleasant to work with, had made much progress, and had openly expressed her gratitude. Again, however, the relevant criterion is the client's best interests: sooner or later this means her independence from the counsellor.

The termination phase should begin with the counsellor, and whenever possible the client, reviewing and summarising what has happened in counselling. There could be reference to both the original goals and the results, and also to the time that has elapsed. An appropriate note to end on could be the counsellor's preparedness to continue on a 'call-me-if-you-need-me' basis, coupled with his indicating that he expected not to be contacted because he had faith in her ability to cope.

Summary

Motivating clients to take action to solve problems should be every counsellor's goal. This means that counsellors should be effective teachers, helping clients to choose and commit themselves to taking action in circumstances where success is virtually assured. Major changes may take time, but as soon as possible clients should be encouraged to try some new patterns of behaviour.

6
Consultation

One-to-one remedial counselling is limited in its scope to the problems of an individual. However, through consultation, a counsellor can reach more people, contribute to institutional change and assume a preventive role.

Consultation is a helping process whereby the counsellor-consultant uses her skills to deliver an indirect service to clients. The consultant works with the key personnel in an organisation to advise them on how to help particular clients or how to change the system in ways which will help individual members in it. Through training and self-awareness the counsellor has skills in communication and interpersonal relationships which equip her to act as a good model and to deal with the feelings that arise when changes are instituted.

An example of consultation would be a school principal calling on a psychologist to diagnose a pupil's problem and advise the teacher on how to deal with it. In this situation it is essential that the psychologist-consultant obtain accurate and full information from as many sources as possible. She may directly observe the client in the setting of concern or arrange for some third person to systematically record teacher-pupil interactions.

It is essential that the consultant communicates clearly with the principal and teacher so that they understand her role and their roles, how she assesses the problem, what actions she sees as feasible and what outcomes can be expected. It is also most important to check on progress and evaluate the final outcome.

Through the consultation process the psychologist-consultant shares her expertise by modelling, and involving the teacher in, the processes of problem-definition, generation of solutions and evaluation of results. Indirectly she 'treats' an individual client by allowing a teacher to be in direct control of the helping process. The teacher selects the methods he thinks are the most appropriate from those suggested, he determines the best timing, he carries out the treatment, and he decides when he is satisfied.

Other instances of this type of consultation are a counsellor consulting with a parent about a disobedient teenager, with a wife about an alcoholic husband or with an employee about a domineering supervisor.

Another type of consultation involves the provision of an expert service in response to a consultee's diagnosis of a problem. For example, a factory manager may feel that his foremen lack skill in communicating with the workers under their supervision. A school principal may want to appoint deans or tutors within a pastoral care network but may feel that the teachers selected need some training before undertaking their new role. In both situations a counsellor-consultant could provide training in communication or human relationship skills. Such training is in demand in church and education groups, commercial, industrial and retailing firms and voluntary social agencies as well as in the professional helping services.

What follows is an outline of the vital issues in running such courses and a sample course.

Teaching Counselling Skills

While counselling skills are transferable to a wide range of situations, a counsellor contemplating acting as a consultant by teaching a skills course should be thoroughly trained and proficient first. However, the preparation of, and leadership of courses can sharpen the counsellor's awareness and performance. Such teaching becomes a form of group counselling for the participants in the training courses. Participants have personal goals in entering into training and they have the opportunity for open sharing of feelings and honest feedback. They can grow in self-awareness and in understanding of others through the relationships established during the training. Such learning, of course, is also open to the training course leader as she receives feedback from participants. She should make it clear that she, too, is willing and expecting to learn.

Leaders of Training Courses

A high level of maturity and interpersonal competence is required in those who lead training groups. On the personal level it is desirable that the leader be warm, open, self-accepting and able to reveal herself. She should be able to refrain from dominating and to allow participants to take the initiative. It is important to be flexible and able to change the programme if this is appropriate. The leader needs to be trained, experienced and proficient in a wide range of skills. Her use of language will be particularly important. It is highly desirable to begin as a sort of apprentice to an experienced leader.

The setting and the composition of the group need to be considered when choosing a leader. Someone who is excellent in an academic setting may not be as effective in communicating to housewives. A high-powered personality may be threatening to those beginning to experience human relationships training for the first time. The leader needs to be someone the group can readily trust and with whom they can feel secure.

Undertaking to train others requires a considerable commitment of preparation time, energy and involvement. Those who acquire reputations as good leaders need to beware of accepting too many invitations outside their regular jobs because of the demands of intimate forms of communication. A balance of work and leisure is essential.

A leader may come from within one's own organisation or may be invited from outside. An outside leader may not be as threatening in that she does not have to be faced every day after the course is over. Also, an outsider is not already involved in the complexities of colleague relationships with the participants and does not have to worry about facing them afterwards. An inside leader, on the other hand, will be aware of participant characteristics prior to the course; she may have a more accurate assessment of their level of functioning and their needs; and she is more readily available for follow-up, particularly if the training has raised strong anxieties in any group member. These points need to be considered by the organisation when choosing a leader.

Clarity of Aims and Objectives

It is vital that aims and objectives be clearly specified as a means of structuring and directing a course. Teaching counselling skills demands a high level of leader and participant involvement and is much more difficult than imparting information in a lecture situation. It is very easy to lose or confuse the participants. Clearly stated aims and objectives help to provide a sense of security, direction, purpose and progress, all of which encourage involvement.

In the first place it is necessary for those desiring training to state their aims clearly and precisely. They may need help to do this as their starting point may have been vague. It may take time to get people to state aims but during the process the person who will be their leader can become aware of their stage of development. The following questions may be useful:

1. When, and for how long, are sessions to be held?
2. How many people will be involved?
3. What facilities are available?
4. What sort of training have participants been involved in before, if any?
5. What is the spread of ages and education?
6. What would you hope each participant would learn?
7. What overall effect do you hope for in your organisation?
8. What sort of follow-up, if any, is planned?

The structure of the course, the explanations and the selection of practical exercises should all serve to further the aims and objectives. Otherwise activities may be but pleasant time-fillers. Participants may be invited to prepare for the course by reading certain material, filling in questionnaires or engaging in some form of self-analysis. Finally, when the course is under way, participants are entitled to know the aims of the whole course and the expected learnings from each exercise. Also, they should have the opportunity to provide feedback as to how far the aims and objectives have been achieved. In skills training the emphasis should be on practical exercises with a minimum of theory and a maximum of involvement.

EXERCISE 6.1*

You have been asked to run a course for voluntary social workers on Basic Communication Skills. Precisely state your overall aim.

EXERCISE 6.2*

In the course you have chosen to use the following sorts of exercises. What would be your reasons for using each? In other words, what skills would you expect participants to understand, and be able to use after practice?

1. An exercise in paraphrasing (reflecting content). (See pp. 56-57)

2. An exercise in giving feedback as to the accuracy of a partner's listening after she has reflected feeling. (See pp. 56-57)
3. An exercise in sharing feelings. (See exercise 2.3, p. 23)

Size and Composition of Groups

Various factors need to be considered when deciding on group size. The amount of space available may place a limit on numbers. If physical arrangements are adequate, a group of 20-24 can be handled comfortably by one leader provided the group subdivides where appropriate. Some practical exercises call for pairs, others for trios and yet others for quartets. Experience suggests a group membership of six to ten (with eight the preferred number) is most appropriate for discussions or small group interactions.

When the composition of a group is considered, differences in sex, age, educational level, ability to verbalise and personality may be significant. Drawing attention to issues or problems that may result from these differences can provide effective teaching points for the group leader. If, for example, group members are threatened by the presence of a university graduate, this issue should be revealed and aired. The feelings aroused may be similar to those a client experiences when meeting 'an expert', eg., a counsellor. This similarity can be emphasised to the group.

There seems to be no optimum combination of characteristics. Diversity in the group provides varying points of view. In the end the significant features usually turn out to be the degree of commitment to the training course, willingness to share openly and to change, and the ability to accept and deal with one's own reactions and those of others.

Group Methods

Factors which are appropriate in individual counselling are also important in groupwork. The following rules will serve as guidelines for group leaders.

1. Instructions for any exercise or activity should be clear, eg.:
   'Form groups of three. One group member is to call himself 'A', another 'B' and the third 'C'. During the first exercise 'A' will counsel 'B' with 'C' observing.'
2. The leader should beware of dominating or overtalking. If instructions and explanations are clear and concise, a maximum amount of time can be spent on

practising the skills. An example of an explanation of reflecting content follows:

'Reflecting means restating the client's basic message in similar but usually fewer words. It indicates that you have heard and shows how well you have understood. Look at the example you have been given.' (Leader reads this aloud and discusses it.)

'Of course it would be artificial to paraphrase or reflect constantly, but in these exercises you will be asked to do this as a way of focusing on active, accurate listening.'

3. In the small working groups encourage everyone to participate. These hints may help:
   (a) Before beginning exercises emphasise that for maximum benefit from the course everyone should participate fully.
   (b) Subdivide into pairs or threes. This encourages participation.
   (c) Help silent members to participate by occasionally asking them questions. Be aware of their non-verbal reactions and comment when appropriate.
   (d) Beware of the person who tries to use the group for his own needs, eg., as an audience. Avoid lengthy monologues or dialogues between one member and the leader by:
      (i) Suggesting that a private issue be discussed at another time, eg., 'As it is a personal matter, I suggest that we discuss this over lunch.'
      (ii) Reminding the group of its purpose for meeting, eg., 'That's interesting but at present we are practising reflecting.'
      (iii) Inviting others to participate, eg., 'Let's hear from Mary now' or, 'What do you think, Mark?'
4. Focus on the here and now rather than on the past or events outside the group.
5. Each person should speak only for himself and not for anyone else or the whole group (unless acting as spokesperson), eg., he should try to say, 'I' rather than 'we' or 'they'.
6. Each person is responsible for the consequences of his or her own actions within the group.
7. As far as possible be aware of each person in the group, not just the current speaker. When leading, look at group members other than the speaker.
8. If people keep directing statements to you as leader, redirect them, eg., 'What do the rest of you think?' or, 'What do you think, John?'

9. Be aware of physical movements. They may indicate boredom, frustration, lack of understanding, tension, etc.
10. Accept all feelings without imputing rightness or wrongness to them.
11. Be aware of yourself as a model. As far as possible demonstrate empathy, warmth and trust.
12. When sub-groups are working on exercises, check each group to ensure that members are keeping to the task.
13. If you cannot answer a question, simply say so.
14. Allow the group to decide whether they want the proceedings to be confidential.

Voluntary or Involuntary Membership

This issue in relation to counselling individual clients has already been examined in chapter 3. Voluntary membership is usually preferable. The negative feelings or defensiveness of an involuntary group member may have a powerful dampening effect. If the situation is particularly threatening to the involuntary member, he may even set out deliberately to sabotage proceedings. The involuntary member may also convey his negative feelings to outsiders and thus prejudice them against such forms of training.

Besides the danger to the group there is also potential danger for the involuntary member. A number of people who appear to function well in ordinary life may really be hiding behind a mask. Open sharing in a group may force this mask off and leave the participant without the help and support needed to deal with his feeling of being exposed.

As with the involuntary client in individual counselling, it is important to raise the issue of compulsory participation if the organisation you are helping has insisted on it. We believe that a person with strong negative feelings towards training should be given the chance to withdraw. But, if at the outset the invited leader suggests to the organisation that voluntary participation is preferred, the issue need not arise. Once the course begins, however, voluntary participants may find themselves reacting very defensively because they could not have realised previously the extent to which the activities would be threatening. Such negative feelings should be dealt with as they arise and not be put aside.

The Physical Setting

The physical setting should be as comfortable and relaxing as possible. The room temperature needs to be warm enough for comfort but not so warm that it will send everyone to sleep. There should be as little as possible outside interference in the form of extraneous noise or interruptions. Traffic noise or noise from other rooms that are not sound-proofed can be distracting. A carpeted or carpet-tiled room, comfortable chairs, plenty of space and withdrawal areas for small groups are all conducive to a good course atmosphere. If possible, participants should be free from all other calls on their time during the course. It is helpful if tea-making facilities are available so that during informal socialising at breaks, course members can relax and shed some of the tensions that may have arisen or share their enthusiasm over new learning.

Timing and Length of Course

Experience suggests that courses lasting two to three days have more impact than those consisting of short sessions spread over a number of weeks. There is enough time for rapport to be developed between the leader and participants and among the participants themselves. This gives the course an impetus which is not dispersed in the way it would be if there were a week's gap between sessions. Participants tend to be fresher and therefore more able to learn if a course is held in the daytime rather than in the evenings, tacked on to a day's work. This also applies to leaders. During a full day, breaks every one-and-a-half to two hours are needed.

Ideal conditions may not be possible. If the course is spread over a number of weeks, one-and-a-half to two-hour sessions are probably long enough, especially if held in the evenings when 7.30-9pm seems a useful time. Another aspect of timing to be considered is placement of the course among the other commitments and stresses of participants' lives. If course members are withdrawn from work at a time of seasonal pressure, both they and their fellow-workers may react negatively. Similarly, try to avoid a time when everyone is tired.

Materials

The choice of materials will be determined by the aims of the course, the selection of activities to promote these aims, the amount of money available and the ease of access to facilities for filming or printing, and so on. There can be a temptation to use audio-visual aids to appear up-to-date or novel rather than because they suit your purpose. The key questions in deciding to use audio-visual aids are:

1. What would best suit my purpose?
2. How available are these materials?
3. Am I competent to use them or is technical assistance on hand?

Videotapes and audio-tapes are powerful aids in the teaching of counselling skills but they can cause annoyance if the operator is unfamiliar with the equipment or it has not been checked to see if it is working. Sometimes, too, the effort required to obtain and operate these devices is too great to be warranted. The use of audio-visual aids increases rather than diminishes preparation time. Careful planning is required, otherwise the audio-visual aids will be mere gimmicks.

It is helpful to have exercises printed beforehand but they can be presented on overhead projector transparencies, on large sheets of newsprint or on a blackboard. Participants can be asked to bring pens and paper but it is wise to provide some for those who forget. They may also receive directed reading material to use for preparation prior to the course.

Follow-up

For maximum benefit it is valuable to have some form of follow-up. The new learnings are reinforced by subsequent practical work and discussions. Without follow-up the effects of a course may last for only a few weeks while the enthusiasm produced by the course remains.

Follow-up may take the form of one or a series of short meetings. During these, participants may share experiences in using the skills learned, seek support or further direction, or request help in extending their skills. As some courses may gather people from distant places, follow-up via a newsletter, further directed reading, a written sharing of experiences or having district contacts available to answer queries may be helpful. The effectiveness of the course could be assessed by attempting to survey its influence on the subsequent fieldwork of participants.

Another form of follow-up is for participants to report back to their colleagues, or, once they have the experience and confidence, to teach others in their organisations. Again, course members can be made more aware of other, more extended, training courses in their area and encouraged to attend them. Follow-up is vital to strengthen the impact of a course and to stimulate on-going learning.

Sample Course

This course is offered as an example.

BASIC COUNSELLING SKILLS

Purpose

To train teachers to function as tutors in a guidance network.

Aims

1. To make the tutors aware of the boundaries of their role.
2. To develop active, empathic listening skills.
3. To practise effective responding.

Length

An introductory session of one hour after school followed by two whole days with three sessions per day, each of approximately one-and-a-half hours with breaks for morning tea, lunch and afternoon tea.

Setting

A school library with carpet tiles and comfortable chairs.

Equipment

Printed handouts.
Four cassette tape-recorders.

Outline

Session 1. A discussion to define the tutor's role. The aim was to help tutors to recognise their place in the total guidance network, to realise the limits of their role, to assess their strengths and weaknesses and to define their needs for training.

Session 2. Exercises to develop active, empathic listening.

(a) Sentence completion in pairs with the listening partner repeating the speaker's message and asking for feedback as to accuracy. (See chapter 2 exercise 2.3) This was designed to focus on accurate listening with the listening partner providing immediate feedback as to accuracy.

(b) Exercises involving reflection. Participants wrote, spoke and taped responses to client statements. Again the focus was on accurate listening in which nothing was added or taken away from the essential message. (See chapter 4 pp. 55-57)

Session 3. Identification of feelings from written statements. (See exercise 4.1) The aim was to help tutors accurately perceive and respond to expressions of feeling, as this is a significant way of conveying acceptance to a client.

Session 4. Role-playing typical tutor-client interviews in pairs before observers, and subsequent discussion. This session was aimed at allowing tutors to experience typical tutoring situations and then critically examine them. They could see various types of interactions and assess their effectiveness.

Session 5. An exercise in listening and response styles. This exercise allowed tutors to recognise five types of response (evaluative, interpretative, supportive, probing, understanding), to find out whether they had a particular pattern of responding, and to evaluate the effectiveness of their responses.

Session 6. An examination of responsibilities, resources and referral. This provided an opportunity to take a detailed look at the tutors' place in the total guidance network.

Session 7. A demonstration interview and summing-up. The aims were similar to those in session 4. The summing-up emphasised the need for further training.

The Counsellor as a Staff Member

The counsellor may work as part of a team that includes psychologists, social workers, medical personnel, teachers or management. It is important to define roles clearly and to work within these definitions, respecting the rights of colleagues.

Some relationships within an agency will be hierarchical and the counsellor may be subject to the authority of a person, such as a principal, who is not trained in counselling. Acceptance of a position within the agency presumes acceptance of its authority structure.

To be seen as authentic within her organisation, a counsellor, in her relationships with her colleagues, should model desirable counselling qualities. That is, she should show warmth, empathy and respect for others. She should be prepared to disclose herself as a person with strengths and weaknesses. She needs to be prepared to listen to other points of view, honestly face conflicts and, where necessary, accept workable compromises.

As a staff member the counsellor may function as a consultant to fellow members of the staff team. This may take place within a discussion about an individual during which the counsellor-consultant mediates as data is pooled, the problem defined, interventions decided upon and roles assigned. The client receiving the indirect service could be a difficult pupil who appears to be disruptive, or a worker who appears depressed. The counsellor can facilitate the case discussion by using skills such as active listening, paraphrasing, focusing and summarising. She can also contribute her knowledge of possible interventions and of support services.

The counsellor may also act as a consultant by collaborating with colleagues as equals to define and solve problems. In a school this could involve setting up a withdrawal room, planning a parent education course, or planning and implementing a study skills programme.

Alternatively, the counsellor-consultant may act as a resource linker, putting other staff in touch with needed materials or people.

The principles of consultation can also be applied to the supervision of a fellow-professional such as a teacher, a nurse, a social worker or a psychologist. Should such a person wish to perform some aspect of his job better, a counsellor with experience as a consultant could help him to achieve this through supervision. The counsellor usually has the advantage of having no administrative power over her fellow-professional, and is thus able to reduce the anxiety that is often present in supervision. She can act as an expert observer, model effective skills and relationships, and may thus improve the practice of supervision within the organisation.

Many aspects of administration and management can also be improved by applying the principles of consultation.

Essentials in Consultation

1. Trusting, supportive, non-judgemental, open relationships.
2. A minimum of threat to the consultees.
3. Full and accurate information correctly communicated.
4. Negotiation between participants which should lead to commitment to the goal.
5. Involvement of participants in all stages.
6. Clear definition of the problem, interventions and projected outcomes.
7. Acceptance of the potential consequences.
8. Evaluation of results.

Summary

Consultation, the provision of an indirect service to clients, widens the counsellor's sphere of influence, allows others such as teachers or foremen to learn new ways of dealing with problems, and may lead to institutional change. The counsellor-consultant may diagnose and prescribe remedies for a problem, she may run a skills training course, she may convene a case conference, or she may meet as an equal with other staff members to define a need and plan for organisational change. Consultation provides an effective way of sharing a counsellor's skills and can have a preventive rather than a remedial emphasis.

7

Other Issues in Counselling

Value Questions

Should One Counsel?

Before beginning to counsel, one may well have to ask whether counselling is appropriate in the particular situation with which one is faced. Other means of helping, eg., music, drama, physical activity, medication or meditation may be more suitable. The key considerations in deciding whether to counsel or not are the client's welfare and her rights. The client's wishes are paramount, but if she is a juvenile or if her life or physical health are at risk, it may be necessary to over-rule her wishes.

Counsellors must recognise that helping one person to change may alter family relationships and result in intolerable pressures being placed on that person to resume her former role in the family, eg., that of symptom-carrier or scapegoat. Counsellors should be cautious about altering family patterns because what is done to one person is likely to affect others. They should also be cautious because to many clients they will represent very different moral, religious or socio-economic positions. It is possible for a forceful counsellor inadvertently to influence a client to accept something she really does not desire.

As well, counsellors aspire to high levels of personal functioning which others may not choose, nor be able, to reach. A counsellor may be asking a client to cope with tremendous mental pain. In a sense the process may resemble an operation. Adults have the right to choose to accept or reject surgery after the situation has been explained to them. Clients seeking counselling should have a similar right.

Counsellor Values

Values may be thought of as the 'oughts', the ideals on which decisions are based. They are an indispensable part of reality. All individuals behave in accordance with a set of values, whether these have been thought out and made explicit or not. Therefore, a counsellor cannot maintain a position of neutrality.

Counsellors will be concerned with four types of values: moral, social, legal and spiritual. Moral values are concerned with concepts of good and evil and often find expression in social values. We may subscribe to the idea that love is good and express this socially in upholding the institutions of marriage and the family. The law may then support these values by regarding marriage as a legal contract, not to be broken easily, and by protecting children through laws relating to custody and maintenance. When these values are placed in a larger context, such as consideration of the meaning and purpose of life, the spiritual dimension exists.

Again, counsellors will be involved in value questions of varying levels of importance. Respect for life is a high-level value, while conventions of dress and housekeeping are not so vital ultimately, although some people behave as if they were.

Are there any basic values to which society can expect counsellors to subscribe? In the section on the counsellor's personal qualities in chapter 2, a number of desirable counsellor characteristics were suggested, among them acceptance of others, open-mindedness, respect for others, self-awareness and objectivity. It is reasonable to assume that underlying such qualities are the basic values of tolerance, concern for others, recognition of the worth of each individual, belief in oneself, honesty, truthfulness, goodwill and caring. These values are widely accepted as essential to community life, and, because of its nature, the counselling relationship demands that counsellors hold these values.

In an increasingly divergent society the counsellor may find himself at variance in values and lifestyle with some of his clients and with sections of the community, particularly on controversial issues such as sexual behaviour, contraception, abortion, drug use, energy conservation and racial attitudes.

The counsellor usually works within institutional limitations. Each agency, preferably explicitly, but sometimes only implicitly, has its boundaries within which the counsellor is expected to function. A church counselling agency may insist that its counsellors be committed Christians and that the spiritual dimension be an essential part of any counselling. A school may insist on the right of parents to know that their children are receiving counselling and may place age limits on certain types of counselling, especially where there are laws to consider, as in the matter of discussing contraception with students under a certain age.

Often then, the counsellor is placed in situations of value conflict. Values are part of his own identity and he must expect to meet clients from other cultures and subcultures who hold very different values. Differences in age, race and socio-economic status increase the likelihood of value conflicts. For example, a counsellor may believe that open sharing of feelings, respecting the rights of others and talking through disagreements are the best ways of working through a conflict. His client, however, may live in a setting where physical violence is the usual method of settling arguments and anything else is regarded as soft.

Society's expectations of the counsellor's role, especially in the counselling of juveniles, may cause value conflicts for a counsellor. What of the counsellor facing a 16-year-old school girl who is living with a 32-year-old separated father of two? The client's concern may be to cope with the stresses associated with this situation while choosing to remain in it, but the parents', the school's and society's expectation probably would be that the counsellor would attempt to persuade the girl to terminate this relationship.

A third value conflict situation is that already implicit in the counsellor's placement within an agency which has certain boundaries to its role, especially if it is a state agency. Where a social worker is investigating an adoption or fostering placement, she may be convinced of the personal qualities of the prospective parents but their home may not meet the physical criteria. A school often expects guidance counsellors to persuade academically able pupils who are resistant to attending university to change their minds.

Where there are inconsistencies among a client's values, the counsellor's role is clearer: he should confront the client with the inconsistencies, and thus help her to clarify her values. However, this can still be difficult. A very aggressive client may appear to value her child's well-being in seeking help with his management but may then, by refusing to co-operate, reveal her true position which is rejecting of him. It takes courage to confront such a client with her true values. If this is done, it might then even be necessary for the counsellor to withdraw from the case.

The counsellor may also meet clients who have contravened society's standards or broken laws. There can then be a conflict between the counsellor's duty to his client and his duty to society, especially where serious crimes are revealed, eg., serious drug offences, extensive theft, hit-and-run driving or even murder. How then can the counsellor cope with the value conflicts that will be an inevitable part of his work?

It is not possible to give specific directions but the following general guidelines can help.

1. Each person has the right to follow his or her own conscience.
2. To remain true to himself the counsellor cannot divorce himself from his own social, moral and spiritual values. He has a right to them. But he must know himself, recognise his values and be honest about them.
3. His task is to help the client rationally examine her values, make her own decisions (preferably avoiding harmful extremes), and establish her own identity.
4. Young people are particularly quick to see through phoney values and to challenge double standards. The counsellor should honestly recognise the justice of some allegations by clients rather than defend the institution and his colleagues automatically. It may be possible to teach the client appropriate ways of challenging the system.
5. The counsellor does not have the right to impose his own values on clients.
6. His position is not that of judge; his function is not to assign guilt or innocence but to encourage objective evaluation of attitudes, standards and actions.
7. Many clients have an expectation and fear of being judged. They already feel guilty because of having contravened their own, their family's or society's moral code. It does not help to deny the reality of this conflict by suggesting that there is no need to regard their behaviour as deviant.
8. A counsellor does not operate in isolation. He is usually a type of social agent, expected to work within the law and basic values of society. His boundaries may be reasonably narrow and defined by statute as in the case of social workers in a government department, or they may be wide as in the case of detached youth workers. However, at some stage a decision as to how much can be accepted will have to be made.
9. If there is any place for judgement, it should be actions rather than persons that are judged.

Values questions are central to the counselling process.

Confidentiality

The client's right to confidentiality is regarded as basic because the counselling relationship is an intimate one based on trust. Confidentiality means keeping secret any information concerning the client which she has revealed in counselling. Unfortunately, absolute confidentiality is probably rare because of human fallibility, staff discussions, and inter-agency sharing, or client permission to divulge information.

Most clients divulge information about their situations, their past, and their innermost feelings in the belief that they are sharing confidences, because this is necessary if help is to be obtained. They trust the counsellor with such information, assuming it will remain confidential. Within limits, confidences must be respected.

We suggest the following guidelines:

1. The client should know where she stands in relation to confidentiality. For example, if case discussion is routine within an agency, the client should be told this.
2. Where referral to another agency or consultation with another family member seems appropriate, the client's prior permission should be sought.
3. When a client specifically requests confidentiality regarding a particular disclosure, this must be respected.
4. Where confidentiality has to be broken because of the law or because of danger to the client's life, she should be informed as soon as possible.
5. Records of interviews should be minimal, noting only what is essential within the particular agency setting. Records should be locked up, shared only with authorised recipients who would also be bound by confidentiality, and destroyed when the counselling relationship is terminated.
6. An atmosphere of confidentiality is even more important than any verbal assurances of it. If, for example, during the interview notetaking is considered essential, the counsellor could offer to let the client see what is being written or even write it herself. Confidentiality then takes on a new meaning for her.
7. Confidentiality, when part of a professional code of ethics, should be upheld.

Physical Contact

Another ethical question relates to physical contact between counsellor and client. Some counsellors say that they sometimes hold a client's hand, or put an arm around a client's shoulder, or even embrace a client. The question is whether such behaviour is ethically and professionally justified as a means of helping clients.

Physical contact between counsellor and client is more acceptable in some institutions, such as hospitals, than in others, such as schools. Even within an institution it is more justified in some situations than in others, such as an interview resulting in much emotional upset compared with one involving only rational discussion. Finally, in some counsellor-client pairings physical contact seems to be more accepted than others, for example a woman counsellor with a girl client compared with a man counsellor with a girl client. Although norms are changing, women counsellors may still be seen more naturally and effectively to initiate such contacts with both males and females.

In many circumstances a client may well be helped towards solving her problems (the purpose of counselling) by physical contact with her counsellor. On the other hand, there is still something of a risk in physical contact in non-medical settings. The following may be the crucial question: when the issue of physical contact arises, how will the client's needs be served by such contact?

Other Settings

In this book counselling skills have been described in ways which assume a one-to-one relationship in which, without pressure of time, a client is helped directly with her own problem. Those who help clients in different settings will probably still find useful many of the skills that have been presented. In this section some other settings are discussed briefly. Those who work in them should consult the bibliography for further discussion.

Political Activity

A radical view of counselling suggests that in some circumstances the most effective way of helping clients might have little to do with counselling and more to do with political activity. Giving help through political activity means no more than bringing about those changes in individuals and organisations which lead to the relief of distress for clients. Nevertheless it represents for many counsellors a considerable change in thinking.

Take, for example, a counsellor in a small voluntary organisation trying to help people who need assistance from a welfare agency which has very complicated ways of dealing with applications. The counsellor may well reach the point of deciding that he would help more by altering the unreasonable policies and methods of the agency, than by continuing to show his clients how to fill in agency application forms. Many other examples could be cited. Community workers could teach people who feel powerless how to organise themselves into a group and then how to get their grievances heard and acted upon. A school counsellor might work to alter unreasonable rules. A social worker in a large government department could try to simplify some procedures. A personnel officer might find a better way for employees to make complaints.

Counselling skills are useful in such situations, but different orientations and procedures should also be adopted. These include:

1. To be successful in his political activity the counsellor will often find it necessary to be more assertive than is usual in counselling.
2. Both orally and in writing, he should express proposals forcefully but not offensively.
3. He should keep detailed records. These pay dividends in supporting proposals.
4. He should tailor every proposal to a particular audience.
5. The counsellor should develop a good sense of timing.
6. Before important meetings he should mobilise support and anticipate the nature and strength of objections to his ideas.
7. He should be prepared to tolerate both his own anxieties and the aggression of others, which are inevitable parts of the process of change.

Working with Groups

A group is a collection of people in which members are aware of themselves as individuals and of others as members of the group and in which there is some common reason for participation.

In most cases counselling with small groups of clients with similar needs and problems is just as effective as that done individually. While there are certain limitations to group counselling, there are also many advantages over the one-to-one setting:

1. The counsellor's time and skill are used more economically.
2. The setting is more natural and realistic than the individual interview.
3. The client sees that her problems are not unique.
4. She has direct opportunities to observe alternative ways of handling problems and the consequences of doing so.
5. A reasonably secure setting is provided in which she can try new behaviours.
6. Through helping others, she is better able to accept help from others.
7. The group's power in interpreting norms to the client makes it difficult for her to continue behaving in negative ways.
8. The reality and immediacy of the group increases the effectiveness of discussion.
9. Tension can be relieved.

Every counselling group has two purposes:

1. To accomplish a particular job eg., to learn social skills; to promote professional development.
2. To sustain itself by meeting the needs of its members, in particular their emotional needs.

Whether there is one designated leader or whether members share the leadership role, the use of certain skills facilitates group functioning. Use of skills such as arranging introductions, giving information, clarifying, expanding a statement, summarising and testing group unity helps the group to achieve its purpose. Encouraging, helping the group to resolve conflicts, facilitating participation (see chapter 6, page 98, number 3 for suggestions), compromising and setting standards, are skills which help the group sustain its emotional life and accomplish its tasks. Another essential leadership task is to help the group review what it is doing from time to time.

Whatever the purpose of the group, its objectives are more likely to be achieved and members' satisfactions are likely to be higher if the leader recognises that there are stages in the development of groups. These stages are very like the three described for individual counselling: a beginning phase, a maintaining and developing phase, and a phase in which plans are made and carried out.

During the beginning phase tentative testing of relationships starts. There are attempts to clarify the nature of the group, the member's place in it, the leader's role and the topics for discussion. In the second phase the group tests boundaries, members try out roles, and a way of working is negotiated. The final phase is characterised by intense communication, expression of emotion and production of solutions. It ends with a separation sub-phase during which participants reinforce each other for contributing to the warmth and depth of the group life and then cope with letting go. Established groups can concentrate on the third phase, but newly formed groups usually need time and competent leadership before working effectively.

Some basic rules help groups to function well:

1. In general it is more productive to deal with the present than with history.
2. So that trust can be maintained members should not repeat personal details about a group member to people outside the group.
3. Each participant is free to decide to what extent he or she will reveal personal details.
4. Each person is responsible for his or her own behaviour in the group.
5. Each person is encouraged to speak for himself or herself but not for another group member or the whole group.
6. Members should accept rather than judge other group members' feelings.

A group is more likely to work effectively if relationships are warm, accepting and non-threatening, and if group members are prepared to co-operate in learning about themselves, other people and how a group works. All members should make a commitment to attend regularly and all should feel free to share in the leadership. The experience should be challenging and worthwhile. Finally, evaluation of what the group has done should play an integral part in the group process.

A member can contribute to effective group work by offering ideas, information or opinions, by disclosing feelings, by listening intently, by encouraging others, by giving and receiving feedback and by being prepared to share in leadership. A designated leader should not only pay attention to the content of any discussion but should also be sensitive to the group atmosphere and the feelings of individuals. He will start the discussion, perhaps, by arranging seating and making introductions. Then he will help the group to clarify its operating rules, facilitate discussion without controlling or dominating it, ask questions and interpret responses, and help the group to assess its progress.

A counsellor should regard the individual skills described in previous chapters as his main resource for working with groups. When acting as a group leader, he will contribute directly by modelling and using these skills. Immediacy may be used as an example. If progress seems to be blocked by undercurrents of feelings, the leader might say, 'I feel frustrated right now and sense that there's some resistance here. I'm wondering from your last comment, Tom, whether you're annoyed about our procedures?' By referring openly and calmly to feelings of annoyance and then asking a member directly to give his reaction, the leader has cleared the way for others to express their feelings. As in individual counselling, open discussion of feelings and procedures in a group is rarely a waste of time.

If structured exercises such as simulation games are to be used, the leader needs to be aware of the following points:

1. Structured exercises are merely devices to encourage learning. Their value for the group lies in the interactions and subsequent discussion generated by them rather than in the exercises themselves.
2. Activities should be selected to suit the interests, needs and abilities of the group.
3. With structured exercises, the reading and oral ability of group members should be taken into consideration.
4. It is helpful to progress from less threatening or less emotionally demanding exercises to those which involve greater personal risk.
5. Variety in the exercises is desirable.
6. While the group is engaged in a structured exercise or during general discussion it may be helpful to appoint one or two group members to act as observers. They may simply record the number of contributions each member makes or they may list behaviours which helped the group to function and those which did not. Alternatively, they may focus on specific behaviours such as eye contact, interruptions or procedural suggestions. Such observations can form the basis of fruitful group discussion.

The main difference between individual counselling and working with groups is that the group leader may have to deal with individuals bidding for power and status and also with sub-groupings whose size, strength and motivations may not be fully apparent. If these factors seem to interfere with the work of the group, again the leader should not avoid the issue but talk openly about his perceptions of what is going on, and then ask for feedback. It is especially important that the leader be seen not to side with one person or faction. He should be at pains to refer to the group's goals and to the importance of first recognising differences, and then work towards them openly, rationally, and equitably.

Families

Work with families constitutes a special type of group work. An important part of each client's life is her family: this may mean only one other person, it may mean a large or small group with whom she lives or it may mean relatives living at a distance. A client can often be better understood by seeing her interacting with her family, or by having her talk about her family. To change a client's outlook or behaviour it may even be necessary to work with her and her family together. It usually takes time to discover what influences are at work in a family, and counsellors who usually work with individuals should become conscious of some features of family relationships.

1. Interactions among members may be on widely differing bases, eg., habitual, economic, supportive, sexual, persuasive, joking.
2. Families use different methods to resolve conflicts, eg., problems may be dealt with openly, immediately, and more or less completely, or they may be solved only partially, leaving unresolved feelings as 'unfinished business'.
3. A certain amount of role-playing and role-taking is inevitable in every family, but sometimes the roles adopted by or given to some members are so fixed that it becomes difficult for them to change, eg., clown, invalid, rebel, boss.
4. In most families members relate to one another as though they were parts of a system. Usually when one member seeks help and is relieved of strain, others feel an increase in strain.
5. It can be helpful to note how rule-making and rule-enforcement are settled in a family. Useful insights can also be gained by noting the operating rules. Some rules are followed and openly talked about (eg., he has one night out a week); some are not talked about but are invariably followed (eg., she never drives the car when he's in it); some may be evident to any outsider but would probably be denied by those concerned (eg., she makes the major decisions).

Provided that he appreciates such factors, a counsellor will find uses for most of the individual skills described earlier. Consider the case in which an apparently weak member of a family is exerting undue power over others by withholding information or refusing to discuss certain topics. It may need the intervention of an outsider using confrontation to help the family to cope with the situation. In a divided family the counsellor's objectivity and refusal to be drawn into coalitions is important, because this forces the members to deal with one another differently. When this occurs, the use of reflection techniques can have powerful effects, causing members to re-think situations.

The counsellor should seize on positive features whenever he can, and then try to define problem relationships in new ways. If change is to occur, it is helpful if relationships are defined differently from the definitions the family has commonly used.

As in individual counselling, new behaviours are important. The family's gaining insight into its own functioning is usually less helpful than simply getting some members to act differently, even in quite small ways, for instance, a weak member might be trained to say 'No' for once; one who wants more say in money matters could be encouraged to spend a small sum on a non-essential item; a quiet person could be urged to start talking about a non-threatening topic.

Family problems usually show as breakdowns in communication. Sometimes this is due to an absence of suitable models: some people cannot imagine family members disagreeing without the interchange sinking into fruitless argument. Many other factors may contribute to poor communication in a family. One parent may have a pressing problem; both parents may have rigid and unrealistic ideas about children's behaviour or school work; there may be understandable worries about adolescents' experimenting with cars, alcohol, and sex; some may have strong desires to control young people's careers or religious beliefs. It is not for the counsellor to decide on the rights and wrongs of such issues, but he may be able to help the family to find solutions.

Where communications are unsatisfactory, the counsellor can help a great deal by directing all members to talk to one another in new ways. It is best if he does this by intervening when the whole family is present and members are actually trying to talk to one another about a problem. Essentially, the counsellor interrupts to give directions in the form of simple rules. He asks that all members, without exception, follow these rules every time they want to sort out a difficulty with others in the family.

The following rules are often useful:

1. Do not talk *about* people who are present: talk *to* them, look at them while you are talking, and use their names.

2. Say what you want to say directly but try to be positive. As well as telling others what you want them to stop doing, say what it is that you would like them to do instead.
3. Whenever possible, talk about problems and feelings as they arise. Tell others how you feel. Do not bottle up feelings of resentment, and do not pretend things are all right when they are not.
4. When others are talking to you, hear them out. Do not interrupt or try to stop them saying certain things. Furthermore, listen carefully to all that is being said to you, especially when the talk is about feelings.
5. Tell others what you like about what they do, as they do it, or as soon as possible afterwards. Emphasise the good things.

Crises

Crises are stressful experiences which are usually sudden or unexpected and which demand almost all of the victim's energy and attention. This sense of preoccupation is heightened by acute emotional distress and at least temporary inability to cope with life's ordinary demands. Crises may be due to loss (eg., divorce), to transitions (eg., new job), or to marked changes in emotional state. Grief as a reaction to severe, prolonged illness or to death is increasingly seen as a special crisis. So too is the immediate prospect of one's own death.

Most adults have grieved and experienced crises themselves and in turn have been called upon to support others in crises. Because of the universality of crises, much of what victims and helpers do at such times are expressions of cultural or sub-cultural beliefs. Thus, much of the support given to and received by victims of severe crises comes through conventional and ritualised forms.

Many people, however, face stressful situations where support from family or friends is insufficient or completely lacking. Counsellors and social workers are often called upon to help in crises where a spouse has run away, a job has been lost, suicide has been threatened, or hospitalisation has been required. More counsellors are specialising in crisis work, such as telephone counselling, drug rehabilitation, legal aid, rape crisis centres, women's refuge centres, citizens' advice centres, and community health agencies. Some organisations working in such settings make special counselling rules, many of which are governed by legal considerations. In their induction courses they give further suggestions to help their counsellors deal with problems they treat in their respective settings.

The judicious use of individual counselling skills serves to help people to cope with crises. However, some special emphases should be noted:

1. Small talk, reassurance and cheerfulness are of little help to clients in crises. Their immediate concern is the urgency and intensity of their problem. Counsellors should likewise focus on these immediate matters and avoid trying to resolve more basic issues.
2. A calm manner is of great value to both counsellor and client. It can be contagious for the client and can help her to focus objectively on her problem. It also serves as a defence for the counsellor against catching the panic that his client feels. In the face of a very distraught client such a manner is difficult to establish, but it can be done if the counsellor's focus is on his client (as it should be) and not on his own fears about his ability to help her.
3. It is important, nevertheless, not to stifle her expression of emotion. The counsellor should help her to deal with her emotions by helping her to identify them, to explore them, to express them, and to come to terms with them. This process often takes a long time. In some crises, notably death, the work of coping with feelings extends over many weeks, and it should not be regarded as just a preliminary to rational planning.
4. At an early stage practical considerations should be attended to. Some of these need to be settled immediately. Is the client or anyone else in physical danger, or in need of food, medical aid, clothing, shelter, money? What resources for help can be mobilised from community agencies and friends and relatives? Are there legal, religious, or other matters to be attended to?

The following suggestions may be useful for the counsellor helping a client in a crisis:

1. Listen carefully to what the client is saying.
2. Communicate your concern and willingness to help.
3. Focus only on the present crisis.
4. Use direct language, eg., 'convicted of assault' rather than 'got into a bit of bother'.
5. Help her to sort the problem into manageable parts.
6. Help her to decide what needs to be done.
7. Encourage her to consider alternatives and weigh consequences.

8. Assist her to choose a limited and attainable goal.
9. Discuss with her any feelings she may have about resisting action.
10. Encourage her to do things for herself.
11. Point out that positive action, however small, brings better feelings.
12. Make further contacts easy for her by arranging a second one.

Developing Competence

In chapters 3, 4 and 5 various counselling skills were described and practice exercises were provided. However, in progressing through this book counsellors may have felt that it was increasingly difficult to remember and apply everything that had been learned. In addition, they may now feel somewhat unnatural and awkward as they try to implement these skills. It may be reassuring to know that others who have practised a similar skills approach to counselling have reported that training actually seemed to hinder rather than help them at first. These feelings tend to diminish with practice and time. In other words, as a counsellor practises the various skills in real counselling situations, he will begin using them almost automatically and will not be so conscious of his 'performance'. He will begin to develop a personal style that is both comfortable and skills-based.

Trying to focus complete attention on the client is one way of aiding this process. In so doing a counsellor will be more helpful to the client, increase the likelihood of using skills appropriately, and will worry less about what he should be saying or doing. If he can do these things, he will be putting more of his energies into the real purpose of counselling – finding out about, understanding, and helping his client.

Estimating Progress

An essential part of counselling is for the counsellor to be able to assess where he is in the process at any given moment. Counselling, after all, is a purposeful activity that follows a predictable sequence of steps. It is important for both counsellor and client to know what progress has been made and what needs still to be done, if only in very general terms. In this book the process has been divided into three broad stages: (i) beginning and developing a relationship with a client; (ii) maintaining that relationship and helping the client explore, clarify and define her problem; (iii) moving from insight and understanding to practical solutions.

By noting the skills he is using and the types of statements the client is making, and by asking himself certain questions, the counsellor can determine where he and the client are in the counselling process. The skills discussed in chapters 3, 4 and 5 are divided according to their appropriateness and effectiveness in the various stages of the counselling process. Thus, if the counsellor finds himself using mainly responding and leading skills and he judges their use to be appropriate at that time in the counselling relationship, he and the client are probably at the second general stage of the process, ie., helping the client explore, clarify and define.

The counsellor can also use the client's statements as a guide to progress. For example, client statements of a general, somewhat vague nature (eg., 'I'm not really sure – all I know is that I had to talk to someone', and 'Well, what do you think – do I have a problem?') indicate that the process is still at the relationship-forming stage. Client statements that demonstrate an effort to clarify or specify feelings, thoughts, words, situations or alternatives, indicate that the process has advanced to the problem clarification stage (eg., 'No, it doesn't happen all the time, just when I refuse to help out', or 'Sure I'm angry! And it feels good to be able to say it!')

Finally, client statements that indicate an attempt to implement a solution, practise a new behaviour or comment on an actual attempt to change, suggest that the process has reached the third or problem resolution stage (eg., 'Yes, I tried that but it didn't work for some reason', or 'I guess I could try talking less – he might like that').

The counsellor can also determine the present stage of the relationship by asking himself specific questions. Positive answers to the following indicate that the main task of the stage in question has been accomplished. Negative answers mean that there is still work to be done at that stage before progressing.

Developing a working relationship:

1. Does the client trust me?
2. Is the client relaxed in this situation?
3. Is the client able to focus on her concern rather than on me and the newness of this situation?
4. Am I ready to work with this client?

Maintaining the relationship and helping the client clarify her problem:

1. Do we both have a clear understanding of her feelings and thoughts regarding her problem?
2. Has the problem been clearly specified?
3. Are we ready to try to resolve the problem?

Resolving the problem:

1. Does she understand what needs to be done?
2. Can she do what needs to be done?
3. Is she committed to putting this plan into action?
4. Can she cope with a failure?

Evaluating Effectiveness

To be an effective counsellor it is essential to assess overall effectiveness. This includes style and its effect on clients, understanding of specific skills and their uses, and success in helping the client meet her expressed needs. It is necessary for the counsellor to make systematic use of a number of sources besides himself in accomplishing this task.

1. He can use a counsellor self-check inventory to assess his own performance. By thinking carefully about what he did and said, he will become more aware of his style and its effect on others.
2. He can have the client complete an interview or counsellor rating scale, in which she is asked to comment both on the interview as a whole and the counsellor's specific behaviour. This will give the counsellor feedback from the 'consumer' on what she found useful, inhibiting, challenging or supporting.
3. Other counsellors could occasionally observe him by sitting in during an interview or by listening to an audio or videorecording of the session. Their comments and observations could be an invaluable source of helpful information.
4. The counsellor could join a counsellor's organisation and participate in the business and concerns of that group. By so doing he would become acquainted

with others doing similar work, share ideas with them, and think about larger issues facing the helping professions.

5. He could set aside some time each week to read in areas that interest him. He could read both to extend his general knowledge of counselling and knowledge of specific problems or areas of counselling that have special relevance or interest for him.
6. All counsellors have an obligation to their clients to try to improve their professional skills and judgement through in-service training.

Supervision

One additional method of assessing effectiveness which deserves a more detailed discussion is supervision. Counselling supervision is a learning relationship which enables counsellors to identify accurately their strengths and overcome their limitations in the practice of counselling. There are at least four different models for conducting supervision: firstly, supervision as teaching (skills acquisition is the primary goal); secondly, supervision as counselling (personal growth and self-insight are the primary goals); thirdly, supervision as administration (organisational administration and case management are the primary goals). The fourth model can include aspects of each of the first three, however, its focus is the counsellor's survival in an agency (understanding influence, power, and agency politics are the primary goals). All counsellors, experienced or inexperienced, can benefit from all four types of supervision at varying times.

Who should supervise?

Supervision will be of greatest benefit when a counsellor selects an experienced, trained counsellor who has had previous experience as a supervisor. It is important that counsellors select supervisors whom they trust and respect and who will challenge them as professionals. Counsellors should avoid asking someone who would have the dual role of supervisor and immediate superior or evaluator. Neither person should be able to use their position or status to influence or manipulate the other.

Where should supervision take place?

Ideally, supervision should occur in a neutral setting. This serves to emphasise the importance of the supervision process and to minimize interruptions and phone calls.

How often and how long?

Ideally, supervision should occur every week. If this is not manageable, once a fortnight can still provide benefits. The length of each session should be agreed on by the participants, but it is suggested that 45-60 minutes is both manageable and sufficient. How long the supervision relationship is to be maintained should be negotiated before beginning. Both parties should be clear about these issues at the outset.

How is supervision carried out?

While not intended as an ideal model, the approach described has been found to be effective and easy-to-follow even for inexperienced supervisors.

(a) Begin by asking the counsellor what issues he wants to work on. This should include specific directions regarding what the supervisor should listen for and comment on.

(b) Ask the counsellor to give sufficient background information about the topic.

(c) Ask the counsellor for a brief, subjective assessment of the case, issue or work situation.

(d) At this point, if using video or audio recordings of a counselling session, play a portion of the tape. Either supervisor or counsellor can stop the tape when wanting to comment.

(e) Supervisors should help the counsellor focus on actual skills used in counselling, aspects of the relationship in question, the overall trend or direction of counselling, basic issues of trust or understanding.

(f) Counsellors should be encouraged to evaluate themselves, to express doubts or questions about their own behaviour.

(g) Avoid focusing exclusively on the client and details of the case.

(h) At some point during the session, the style and direction of supervision should be checked to make sure it is helpful and relevant to the counsellor.

(i) Terminate each supervision session on a constructive note. Counsellors should be left with clear aims and goals to pursue in their future work.

Should audio or video-tape recordings be used?

While neither is essential to effective supervision, their use enables a more objective and careful examination of what has actually occurred. However, recordings are an aid to supervision, and should not be allowed to become an end in themselves.

How is supervision terminated?

The length of the supervision relationship should be agreed on before the process is actually begun. Both supervisor and counsellor should feel free to terminate supervision if the needs of either are no longer being adequately met.

If counsellors followed these steps in evaluating and improving their own counselling effectiveness, they would not only notice their own improvement in confidence and effectiveness, but would also give more useful service to their clients.

Answers to Exercises

Chapter 3

Exercise 3.1

1. (a) Usually the client will feel most comfortable in position 2.

   (b) Usually the client will feel that the desk is a barrier between him and the counsellor, but some clients may welcome this distancing. Generally, the most welcoming position is that where both client and counsellor are in front of the desk.

2. Generally, position (b) is the most comfortable for clients.
3. Positions (a)-(c) are usually intimidating, but position (d) is welcoming.

Exercise 3.2

All of these situations may be threatening to the counsellor. In each case she first will need to acknowledge the feelings being expressed by the client.

Exercise 3.4

(a) 'You seem very upset. Would you like to tell me about it?'
(b) 'I understand you've been made redundant. How do you feel about it?'
(c) 'What would you like to talk about?' or 'How can I help you?'

Exercise 3.6

1. (b) and (c) are open-ended.
2. (a) What did you enjoy about the party?
   (b) What caused you to leave school?
   (c) What difficulties are there in getting home?
   (d) How did you come by that jacket?

Exercise 3.7

1. You're having difficulty getting a job?
2. You resent this restriction?
3. Can you tell me why?

Chapter 4

Exercise 4.1

1. (a) Begins with 'I feel . . .' but actually describes what the other person does.
   (b) A strong command, but not a description of a feeling.
   (c) Feeling described is 'anger'.
2. (a) Feeling described is 'depressed'.
   (b) No feeling described.
   (c) 'Anyone' – speaker is not speaking for himself. 'Feels less than his best' is too vague.
3. (a) Describes the reaction but not the specific feeling experienced (ie., was it anger, satisfaction, frustration, etc?).
   (b) Merely asks a question. No feeling is specified.
   (c) The first part is a judgement, the second part describes a feeling – 'mad'.
4. (a) Clearly says 'I'm afraid . . . '
   (b) Begins with 'I feel . . .' but no feeling is specified.
   (c) Loaded with feeling but, again, the speaker's feeling is nowhere described.
5. (a) Makes a judgement about another person and self.
   (b) Does not describe a feeling.
   (c) Feeling described is 'relieved'.

6. (a) Merely describes the exercise.
   (b) Feels 'challenged'.
   (c) Ascribes the feeling 'liked' to everyone, not to self.

Chapter 5

Exercise 5.2

1. (a) S; (b) G; (c) G; (d) S; (e) G; (f) G; (g) S; (h) S; (i) G; (j) G; (k) S; (l) S.

Exercise 5.13

Sample Transcript Analysis:

	Skill	**Analysis**
Teacher 1. The problem is this: I have to teach an intensive French course, to cover a year's work in two terms. I'm doing my best, but I can go only as fast as the students can handle the stuff. And on top of this I have to do all the usual administrative things as well. There's just not time for it all.		(Two issues seem to be emerging: not enough time to do everything and feelings about those demands.)
Counsellor 1. You're feeling, then, that what you're being asked to do is just too unrealistic. Is that it?	Reflection of content plus understanding check.	An attempt to highlight the problem, to focus further discussion.
Teacher 2. Yeh. There just isn't enough time. And yet the Principal expects it all to be done. I just think it's impossible. Plus, I don't think she really cares about French.		(Client agrees with reflection and reiterates the problem. The last statement introduces an additional element, possibly feeling-laden.)
Counsellor 2. What are your feelings about that, her not caring about French?	Direct, open question.	Directs by focusing on teacher's feelings about Principal's attitude to French.

Chapter 6

Exercise 6.1

Overall aim. To develop in participants an increased self-awareness and the skills necessary to meet their clients as people, not problems; to convey trust and warmth, to listen creatively, and to communicate clearly.

Exercise 6.2

1. *Paraphrasing:* To enable participants to restate a client's statement in fewer words as an indication of their desire to listen carefully and as a check on the accuracy of their listening.
2. *Giving Feedback:* To teach participants to share their reactions to messages from other people.
3. *Sharing Feelings:* To help participants to identify their own feelings accurately and to share them openly with others.

Select Bibliography

General Counselling

Brammer, L.M. (1979). *The Helping Relationship: Process and Skills.* (2nd ed.) Englewood Cliffs, N.J.: Prentice-Hall.

Belkin, G.S. (1981). *Practical Counselling in the Schools.* (2nd ed.) Dubuque, IA: Wm C. Brown.

Donnelly, F. (ed.) (1981). *A Time to Talk.* Auckland, N.Z.: George Allen & Unwin.

Hackney, H. & Cormier, L.S. (1979). *Counselling Strategies and Objectives.* (2nd ed.) Englewood Cliffs, N.J.: Prentice-Hall.

Ivey, A.E. & Simek-Downing, L. (1980). *Counselling and Psychotherapy: Skills, Theories, and Practice.* Englewood Cliffs, N.J.: Prentice-Hall.

Krumboltz, J.D. & Thoresen, C.E. (1976). *Counselling Methods.* New York: Holt, Rinehart and Winston.

Loughary, J.W. & Ripley, T.M. (1979). *Helping Others Help Themselves: A Guide to Counselling Skills.* New York: McGraw-Hill.

Training of Counsellors

Egan, G. (1975). *The Skilled Helper: A Model for Systematic Helping and Interpersonal Relating.* Belmont, CA: Wadsworth.

Ivey, A.E. & Gluckstern, N.B. (1982). *Basic Attending Skills. (2nd ed.)* North Amherst, MA: Microtraining Associates.

Ivey, A.E. & Gluckstern, N.B. (1976). *Basic Influencing Skills.* North Amherst, MA: Microtraining Associates.

Johnson, D.W. (1981). *Reaching Out.* (2nd ed.) Englewood Cliffs, N.J.: Prentice-Hall.

Okun, B.F. (1976). *Effective Helping: Interviewing and Counselling Techniques.* North Scituate, MA: Duxbury Press.

Training in Social Skills

Manthei, M. (1981). *Positively Me.* (2nd ed.) Auckland, N.Z.: Methuen.

Priestley, P., McGuire, J., Flegg, D., Hemsley, V. & Welham, D. (1978). *Social Skills and Personal Problem Solving.* London: Tavistock.

Trower, P., Bryant, B. & Argyle, M. (1978). *Social Skills and Mental Health.* London: Methuen.

Counselling in Groups

Brownstone, J.E. & Dye, C.J. (1973). *Communication Workshop for Parents of Adolescents: Leader's Guide.* Champaign, IL: Research Press.

Johnson, D.W. & Johnson, F.P. (1975). *Joining Together: Group Theory and Group Skills.* Englewood Cliffs, N.J.: Prentice-Hall.

Miles, M.B. (1981). *Learning to Work in Groups: A Practical Guide for Members and Trainers.* (2nd ed.) New York: Teachers College, Columbia University.

Pearson, K.D. (1975). *RAP Groups: Rapport and Personal Relationships for Youth in Upper Secondary Schools.* Melbourne: Joint Board of Christian Education of Australia and New Zealand.

Consultation

Blake, R.R. & Mouton, J.S. (1976). *Consultation.* Reading, MA: Addison-Wesley.

Boud, D. & McDonald, R. (1981). *Educational Development Through Consultancy.* Guildford, Surrey: Society for Research into Higher Education.

Myers, J., Parsons, R.D. & Martin, R. (1979). *Mental Health Consultation in Schools.* San Francisco: Jossey-Bass.

Prebble, T. & Stewart, D. (1981). *School Development: Strategies for Effective Management.* Palmerston North, N.Z.: Dunmore Press.

Family Counselling

Dodson, L.S. (1977). *Family Counselling: A Systems Approach.* Muncie, IN: Accelerated Development.

Haley, J. (1976). *Problem-Solving Therapy: New Strategies for Effective Family Therapy.* New York: Harper and Row.

Minuchin, S. (1974). *Families and Family Therapy.* London: Tavistock.

Satir, V. (1975). *Peoplemaking.* Palo Alto, CA: Science and Behaviour Books.

Supervision

Boyd, J. (1978). *Counsellor Supervision: Approaches, Preparation, Practices.* Muncie, IN: Accelerated Development.

Hendrickson, D.E. & Krause, F.H. (eds) (1972). *Counselling and Psychotherapy: Training and Supervision.* Columbus, OH: Charles E. Merrill.

Powell, D.J. (1980). *Clinical Supervision: Skills for Substance Abuse Counsellors: Trainee's Workbook.* New York: Human Sciences Press.

Cross-Cultural Counselling

Gadd, B. (1976). *Cultural Difference in the Classroom: Special Needs of Maoris in Pakeha Schools.* Auckland, N.Z.: Heinemann.

Marsella, A.J. & Pederson, P.B. (eds) (1981). *Cross-Cultural Counselling and Psychotherapy.* New York: Pergamon Press.

Metge, J. & Kinloch, P. (1978). *Talking Past Each Other: Problems of Cross-Cultural Communication.* Wellington, N.Z.: Victoria University Press.

Sue, D.W. (1981). *Counselling the Culturally Different: Theory and Practice.* New York: John Wiley.